# GEORGIAN GARDEN BUILDINGS

## Sarah Rutherford with Jonathan Lovie

SHIRE PUBLICATIONS

Published in Great Britain in 2012 by Shire Publications
Ltd, Midland House, West Way, Botley, Oxford OX2 0PH,
United Kingdom.

44-02 23rd Street, Suite 219, Long Island City, NY 11101,
USA.

E-mail: shire@shirebooks.co.uk    www.shirebooks.co.uk

© 2012 Sarah Rutherford and Jonathan Lovie.

Every attempt has been made by the Publishers to secure
the appropriate permissions for materials reproduced in
this book. If there has been any oversight we will be happy
to rectify the situation and a written submission should be
made to the Publishers.

A CIP catalogue record for this book is available from the
British Library.

Shire Library no. 670.    ISBN-13: 978 0 74781 101 5

Sarah Rutherford and Jonathan Lovie have asserted their
rights under the Copyright, Designs and Patents Act,
1988, to be identified as the authors of this book.

Designed by Tony Truscott Designs, Sussex, UK
and typeset in Perpetua and Gill Sans.

Printed in China through Worldprint Ltd.

12 13 14 15 16      10 9 8 7 6 5 4 3 2 1

COVER IMAGE
Detail of Castle Howard Mausoleum.

TITLE PAGE IMAGE
Brizlee Tower, Hulne Park, Alnwick, Northumberland
(Robert Adam, 1777), is said to have inspired the Duke of
Northumberland's pastry cook.

ACKNOWLEDGEMENTS
The authors wish to thank the following for permission to
reproduce pictures:

Jeff Dalton, cover, page 68; Mrs Frances Tilley, page 1;
Buckinghamshire County Museum, pages 4, 5 (left), 9, 15
(bottom), 20 (right), 28 (top), 36 (right), 48 (right), 54,
75, 77 (top), 103, 108 (top); Charles Boot, page 5 (right);
The Landmark Trust, pages 7, 24, 39 (bottom), 114 (top),
118; Bridgeman Art Library, page 8; Bridgeman Art
Library / National Trust pages 17, 47 (right), 53 (bottom
left), 88, 97, 105, 113, 116; John Leverton, page 14; Brian
Hull, page 18; James Holland, page 19; David Burrows,
page 21; Jo O'Callaghan, page 23 (top); Martin Brewster,
pages 23 (bottom), 83 (bottom); Sue Edwards / National
Trust, page 25 (top left); Kelvin Barber, pages 25
(bottom), 27 (top), 36 (left), 38 (bottom), 89, 104 (top);
James Head, pages 28–9; David Hulme, page 34; Ernie
Howard, page 35; Brian Morgan, page 37; The Governors
of Stowe School, page 38 (top); Worcestershire Record
Office, pages 40, 56 (bottom); Lee Henderson, page 43;
originals held at the Somerset Heritage Centre, ref.
DD\L\1/22/7a, used with permission, pages 44 (top), 57
(top), 108 (bottom); Andrew Short / National Trust, page
47 (left); Robbie Phelan, page 48 (left); Russell Butcher,
page 49 (top); Dr and Mrs Paul Stamper, page 52;
Christopher Gallagher, page 55; Peter J. Large, page 65
(bottom); Alex Taylor, page 66 (top left); Tim Davies, page
66 (top right); Kelvin Trundle, page 67; David Oldman,
page 70 (right); Brian Walbey / National Trust, page 72;
Angus W. Murray, page 78; Trevor Morris, pages 81, 91,
92; Adrian Purser, page 84; Philip Masters, page 86; Paul
Thackray, page 96; Mark Wilkinson, page 100; John Ryles,
page 101 (top); Trustees of the Croome Estate, 94
(bottom), and 101 (centre and bottom); Richard Wheeler,
page 107; Ian Docwra, page 109; Jon Exley, page 110;
Damian Entwistle, page 112; Hugh P. Gray, page 114
(bottom).

All other images are from the authors' collection.

The authors would also like to thank Jill Tovey, archivist to
the Croome Estate, and Peter Howell for help and
guidance.

# CONTENTS

# INTRODUCTION

The Wilderness at Hartwell House contained a range of garden buildings in all sorts of evocative styles.

THIS BOOK covers buildings (mainly purpose-built) in landscape parks and gardens of the Georgian period – that is to say, those created during the reigns of the four Hanoverian kings George I to IV (1714–1830). The English landscape garden was a whole new concept pioneered by Georgians and developed during this period as Britain's greatest original contribution to the visual arts. Its influence was immense and it was enthusiastically taken up on the Continent, Russia and in North America.

The Georgian landscape garden and park were populated by a novel and diverse group of buildings in an engaging variety of styles, imbued with literary and Classical associations and allusions. Buildings went up throughout the garden and park, sometimes to our eyes seemingly scattered at random, but in reality they were always placed with care. They were often functional, always ornamental, terminating views and diverting the eye, and usually made a statement about the wealth, education, allegiances and power of their builders. Few of these engaging buildings were just functionless follies.

The key here is the relationship between the building and the landscape design. Georgian garden buildings were not built in isolation but to be seen within the landscape and often as part of a sequence of buildings. They formed part of the design and often also provided a shelter from which to view that design, or fulfilled some other more practical use such as providing a bridge for the drive, a staff house or a farm building. Mainly English examples are offered, with some from elsewhere in the British Isles, including Ireland, which has many exquisite Georgian garden designs and buildings developed in parallel with Great Britain.

Above left:
The Canal Pavilion at Hartwell House in its originally formal setting reminiscent of great French gardens.

Above:
The Canal Pavilion, now overlooks a landscaped paddock and the pavilion remains a shelter and seat from which to observe the landscape.

## ORIGINS

Gardens of the seventeenth and early eighteenth century were formal, similar to French and Dutch styles. From the 1720s formality was gradually replaced by the naturalistic and extensive landscape garden, the greatest exponent of

The pyramid of Caius Cestius in Rome, seen by Georgian Grand Tourists and emulated in their own parks and gardens.

The Pyramid mausoleum at Blickling Hall, Norfolk (Joseph Bonomi, 1794–6), closely resembles that of Caius Cestius.

which was Lancelot 'Capability' Brown (1716–83), as epitomised by his landscaping at Blenheim Palace, Oxfordshire. Plenty of other landscape designers worked in similar manner during the Georgian period, such as Richard Woods (c. 1716–93) and Brown's self-styled successor Humphry Repton (1752–1818). Their employers were owners keen to follow the informal fashion which reduced maintenance costs, replacing gardeners with sheep or cattle to keep the grass down, although latterly the formal flower

garden began to make a comeback. The influence of these landscapers, together with the owners, on the siting and design of garden buildings was seminal.

The Grand Tour of Europe had a profound effect on Georgian garden owners, architects and designers. Their empathy with the past had its major origins in the Civil War of the 1640s and the Commonwealth of the 1650s, when many influential people were exiled to Europe. Initially the Grand Tour was for the education of wealthy young men of good family who sometimes spent several years touring Europe, mainly Italy and other Mediterranean countries which had been colonised by Classical cultures. Their whole education revolved around the antique Classical authors and they could easily relate to the remains and related culture they found.

The golden age of the Grand Tour spread across most of the eighteenth century, from the end of the Duke of Marlborough's wars for Queen Anne (1713) until the French Revolution (1789), when access to Europe was relatively easy. A number of the antique buildings the 'milordi' found in Italy and Greece were often used as models and recorded, published and adapted for garden buildings, together with much antique statuary to people these landscapes. The most popular of these models included Egyptian obelisks, the Tower of the Winds in Athens, and in Rome Trajan's Column, the Arches of Constantine and Titus, the pyramid of Caius Cestius, the Pantheon, and the Temple of Vesta at nearby Tivoli, as well as many other temples and mausolea. Most of these can still be seen as the 'milordi' did, often in very similar surroundings.

The interior of a building, in this case the Bath-house at Walton Hall, was often exquisitely decorated for entertainment and used as a viewpoint for the rest of the landscape and buildings. (See also page 118)

The young, rich Georgians returned to Britain full of enthusiasm for the past and keen to evoke it in their own properties. They discussed their aspirations within new private clubs of their peers such as The Dilettante and Divan societies. The noblemen and scholars of The Dilettante Society sponsored the study of Ancient Greek and Roman art, and the creation of new work in the style. The Society first met in 1732 and was formally established as a London dining club in 1734 by former Grand Tourists. Masonic links were also reflected in gardens but are, especially now, shadowy.

Georgian garden buildings and houses brought home, literally, a sense of physical contact with the Classical past. By 1750 the art and architecture of Classical Greece was becoming better known and a great debate ensued about the merits of Greek art and architecture against Roman. At the same time it became the thing for professional architects to undertake the Grand Tour, such as Robert Adam in the 1750s, although earlier British architects

*Landscape with Aeneas at Delos (1672), a typical landscape by seventeenth-century painter Claude Lorrain that perhaps inspired Henry Hoare's lake scene at Stourhead, Wiltshire.*

had worked in Europe. Another Scot, James Gibbs, had worked in Rome in the 1710s. The influence of Italy and Italian architects, particularly Andrea Palladio (1509–80), himself much influenced by Ancient Rome, pervaded many designs. The antique buildings the Grand Tourists all saw were used as models for many garden and park buildings, particularly the temples and columns. The tourists also saw and were very impressed by the Arcadian landscapes of the seventeenth-century painters Claude, Salvator Rosa and Poussin. Many of these works were acquired, and still hang in the stately homes of Britain; their pastoral idyll is still seen through the windows of their surrounding parks and gardens, such as at Henry Hoare's Stourhead, Wiltshire.

William Kent's Temple of Ancient Virtue, Stowe – an ironic view of the goings on around it by Rowlandson (c. 1805).

Other historical and geographical styles were adopted for garden buildings – mainly medieval northern European Gothic but also Chinese, Indian, Moorish, Ancient Egyptian and what was believed to be Ancient British (called here Druidiana). These styles also evoked associations and ideas in the well-educated few, and several styles were commonly used together in a single landscape design.

Interior and exterior decoration were both essential elements and often the same expert craftsmen were used for exquisite decor in remote garden buildings, as for the country house. Elegant furniture was also designed especially for buildings in some cases.

Pattern books abounded to provide ideas. The best-known examples include James Gibbs's *Book of Architecture* (1728), Batty Langley's Gothic confections in *Gothic Architecture Improved by Rules and Proportions in many Grand Designs* (1747), and Robert and James Adam's *The Works in Architecture of Robert and James Adam* (1778).

The connection of these buildings, their styles, origins and references can be difficult to grasp without explanation, often linked by historical and literary allusions and themes with which we are now unfamiliar. But even without understanding this dimension, these structures are engaging

## DESIGNERS

Robert Adam's design for the London Road gateway, Syon House, Middlesex, published in 1778.

Designers of Georgian garden buildings came from various backgrounds and disciplines.

Outstanding architects designed many of the most important garden buildings, and some designed surprisingly modest ones. The great names include James Gibbs, Sir John Vanbrugh, William Kent, Robert Adam, and William Chambers, who put as much effort into these seemingly minor works as their magnificent country houses and churches.

Landscape designers were often perfectly competent to design garden buildings.

and just as enjoyable for their appearance and contribution to the landscape setting.

Some types of structure overlap between the sections of this book (for example, arches can also be lodges and appear ruined) and some terms are difficult to define firmly because they were loosely used even by the Georgians (for example the blurring between summerhouse, pavilion and gazebo; and gateways and archways). See the glossary on pages 125–6.

Lancelot 'Capability' Brown (1716–83) designed churches (Compton Verney, Warwickshire, 1776), stables (Croome Court, Worcestershire, 1751) and other buildings such as columns for Stowe in Buckinghamshire (late 1740s) and Burton Pynsent, Somerset (1765). Others such as Richard Woods (c. 1716–93) designed garden buildings, notably at Wardour Castle, Wiltshire in the 1760s.

Educated amateurs, both architects and owners, were as important in influence and sheer numbers of garden buildings they designed, and included owners of the highest skill. The great amateur architect owners include Richard Boyle, 3rd Earl of Burlington (1694–1753, Chiswick House, Middlesex), John Freeman (1689–1752, Fawley Court, Buckinghamshire) and Thomas Hope (1769–1831, the Deepdene, Surrey). Other so-called amateurs (because they were not paid fees) advised a wide circle of friends, acquaintances and family, including Thomas Wright (1711–86, the so-called Wizard of Durham), Thomas Pitt, 1st Baron Camelford (1737–93), and Sanderson Miller (1716–80, who also owned and embellished Radway Grange).

The designers of many lesser, and some notable, garden buildings remain shadowy and were probably provincial architect-builders, such as the Hiorn brothers in the Midlands, or

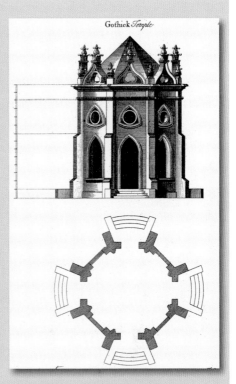

Batty Langley's fanciful Gothick temple design (1747), copied at Bramham Park, Yorkshire.

tradesmen and craftsmen such as mason and carver Thomas Greenway of Bath. They are mostly anonymous because the records relating to their work were not extensive and have survived poorly.

# ARCHES

A S GATEWAYS AND EYECATCHERS, Georgian arches shouted for attention. The grandest arches in Georgian parks and gardens were triumphal arches, full-scale muscular examples based on Roman models. These were used to mark major park entrances (and often double as lodges too) or to commemorate military victories, or sometimes both. Freestanding arches designed purely as park eyecatchers or used as features in the garden were generally less substantial, more affordable, and often two-dimensional. Even so they still had pretensions, usually to the Roman triumphal arch, or sometimes to being a Heaven's Gate where they stood on the skyline. In 1731 the poet Alexander Pope ridiculed those who sought to imitate antique Rome in this way when he wrote of 'imitating fools' who 'turn Arcs of Triumph to a Garden Gate' but this did nothing to dampen the enthusiasm of the landscape improver and many were constructed throughout the Georgian period.

A triumphal arch was, like the monumental column, another landscape building modelled on an antique Roman structure of heroic scale. The originals in Rome itself usually commemorated a victory of the Roman Empire, rather than one man in particular as did the column, but outside Rome, Roman arches were dedicated to emperors and were erected for all kinds of purposes, but they were always commemorative and in honour of someone. Like the column, its chief purpose was to

The Arch of Titus in the Roman Forum (AD 81), was one of three seen by Georgian Grand Tourists. It has similarities with Stowe's Corinthian Arch.

support sculpture, often representing the physical trophies of battle – arms and armour of the vanquished foe – and they would usually have a chariot, bearing the emperor on top.

Examples in British landscape parks and gardens were based on the conspicuous models most easily seen by eighteenth-century Grand Tourists and depicted by artists illustrating Rome, three in particular: the Arches of Titus (AD 81) and Septimius Severus (AD 203) and, grandest of all and frequently copied in British gardens, the Arch of Constantine (*c.* AD 315) next to the Colosseum, with its two smaller arches flanking the main archway. Their basic form and potential for decoration, as the base for sculpture, made them obvious examples for imitation, but they were expensive to build and only for those with virtually unlimited funds unless simplified and narrowed from three to two dimensions.

The Arch of Constantine, Rome, in the Forum next to the Colosseum. It was a popular model for park arches.

Typically, a full-blown triumphal arch stood at the main entrance to the park, furthest from the house to emphasise the extent of the estate: this monumental, three-dimensional structure impressed the visitor at the first opportunity and heralded the wonders of the landscape. If possible it was positioned as an eyecatcher too. It usually straddled the main drive, such as the Woodstock Gate, Blenheim (1723), although the very grand Garendon Arch, Leicestershire (1730s), spanning a more minor drive is an exception. Henry Holland's rather later red sandstone arch at Berrington Hall, Herefordshire, straddles the drive near the house as it enters the pleasure grounds from the park. William Chambers designed the ruined arch at Kew, Surrey, in 1759 for Augusta, Dowager Princess of Wales, as a fully proportioned triumphal arch across a garden path leading around the *ferme ornée*, with a track on top across which to drive sheep and cattle.

The substantial form of the Roman original meant that for park use an arch could be usefully adapted, with rooms, perhaps inhabited by the gate-

Nicholas Hawksmoor's massive Woodstock Gate, Blenheim Palace, opens to the adjacent town. It commemorates the 1st Duke of Marlborough's victories in Europe, and stands prominent in the park.

The Ruined Arch, Kew (1759), by William Chambers, was created for Princess Augusta, Dowager Princess of Wales, and carried a track for sheep and cattle over a garden path. Chambers conceived 'a Roman ruin of antiquity, built of brick, with incrustation of stones' modelled on the Arch of Constantine.

keeper and his family. Stowe's Corinthian Arch (1765–7), apparently floating on a hillside a mile or so south of the vast mansion, must be the largest arch of this sort and is the most dramatic garden building even at Stowe. It did not, however, enamour Thomas Jefferson when he saw it in 1786, for he found that, 'Instead of being an object from the house, it is an obstacle to a very pleasing distant prospect.' At Tyringham, Buckinghamshire, Sir John Soane's stone entrance arch (1794) across the public road into the park was of his typical restrained Classical style, with a small lodge on either side. Kent's great Worcester Lodge at Badminton, Gloucestershire, has two arches, one

The Corinthian Arch at Stowe (1760s), by Thomas Pitt, Lord Camelford, brother of Prime Minister William Pitt the Elder, which frames distant views from the mansion.

The Boringdon Arch, Saltram, Devon (Robert Adam, 1783). It is not an entrance to the estate, but an eye-catcher from the Parkers' newly remodelled house, and the culmination of a circuit of drives through the estate.

Opposite: Hadrian's Arch, Shugborough, Staffordshire, stands on the crest of a hill, framing the sky, its model being the eponymous Roman arch in Athens.

above the other: the lower one of knobbly rusticated stone, flanked by pyramid-roofed pavilions; the upper arch a large, airy banqueting room, in smooth ashlar with a pediment and dome.

Many entrance arches were less substantial and essentially two-dimensional. The architect Robert Adam had something of an obsession with arches. He designed many graceful free-standing arches, such as the London Road Gate, Croome Court, Worcestershire (1779) and the similar Boringdon Arch, Saltram, Devon (1783), which serves as an eyecatcher from the house and a point from which to view the entire landscape design; also the arch and screen at Syon House, Middlesex. Holland designed another screen flanking an entrance arch with arms above for Woburn in 1790. Arches in the garden usually straddled paths and framed views, as Stowe's Doric Arch, and others at Hartwell, Buckinghamshire (now marking a main entrance) and Chiswick, Middlesex, all free-standing and two-dimensional, marking the transition from one part of the garden to another.

Military victories or associations were, naturally, commemorated. At Blenheim Palace, Oxfordshire, the Woodstock Gate (1706–10) commemorates the Duke of Marlborough's 'Defence of Our Liberties' and his victories in the War of the Spanish Succession (including the Battle of Blenheim, 1704). Hadrian's Arch at Shugborough, Staffordshire (1760s), was designed by James 'Athenian' Stuart to commemorate Admiral Lord Anson.

It was based on the Arch of Hadrian in Athens, and embellished with symbolic naval sculpture. The theatrically thin arch at Parlington, Yorkshire (1781–3, Thomas Leverton), stands on the axis of the drive where it turns. Its purpose is evident from the inscription 'Liberty in N. America triumphant'.

As purely eyecatchers, freestanding arches were generally of two dimensions, reminiscent of theatrical scenery, placed on high or other prominent points in the landscaped estate. William Kent's stone eyecatcher (*c.* 1738) at Rousham, Oxfordshire, is a triumphal arch in rusticated form: a simple stone wall with three arches seen against the sky a mile or so distant across the valley from the house. Heaven's Gate, Highclere, Hampshire, is a triple-arched brick eyecatcher for Robert Herbert (built in 1737 and rebuilt after it collapsed in 1739), in the park up on the hill over half a mile from the house and probably designed by his brother Lord Pembroke. It had a seat behind the central arch and rooms for serving tea concealed behind the side arches. Castle Hill, Devon, also combines theatricality and reduced substance. Here the principal southern vista from the house extends about half a mile to the Triumphal Arch (*c.* 1730), also known as Heaven's Gate, an early triple-arched eyecatcher framed on the horizon by woodland.

Opposite:
A narrow 'theatrical' triumphal arch at Parlington, Yorkshire (Thomas Leverton, 1781–3), commemorates the victory of the Americans in the War of Independence.

William Kent's Gothic eyecatcher at Rousham, Oxfordshire, silhouetted on the skyline across the Cherwell valley, over a mile from the Dormer family's house.

# BEASTLY BUILDINGS

Below:
One of James
Gibbs's designs for
a menagerie, from
his 1728 *Book of
Architecture*.

Below right:
The Menagerie,
Hartwell House,
Buckinghamshire
(James Gibbs,
1720s–30s), was
visible from the
house and similar
to the one he
designed for
Hackwood,
Hampshire.

ORNAMENTED BUILDINGS housing animals for farming, sport and as pets were often part of landscape design. These useful follies (perhaps a contradiction in terms) also played their part as eyecatchers or as other incidents in the landscape, perhaps in more intimate surroundings.

Farm buildings ranged from barns, cowsheds, dovecotes and piggeries to sheepfolds and dairies. Sporting buildings covered hound kennels, fishing temples and coops, pheasantries, deer barns and folds, game larders and even cockpits. Pets and zoos were housed in aviaries, menageries, and at Wotton in Surrey there was a house for terrapins. Far from being utilitarian in appearance, this wide range of buildings was suitable for ornamentation in most Georgian styles, the commoner ones being Gothic, Classical and Chinoiserie.

Pattern book designs stimulated owners. James Gibbs in his *Book of Architecture* (1728) published two designs for the menagerie at Hackwood, Hampshire, a solid Classical building with a portico, which was similar to

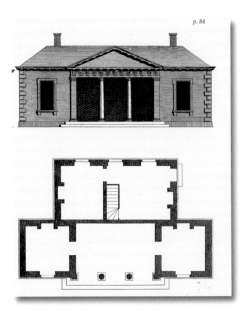

p. 84

that built at Hartwell House, Buckinghamshire, which was later altered. Thomas Wright's Aviary (in *Arbours*, 1755) set a whimsical tone: a rusticated Gothic structure with 'rugged trunks of oak, the more fantastical and robust the better' was decorated inside with ivy-flakes, moss or the roughest bark of oak. John Plaw offered various farm buildings in different styles, in *Ferme ornée or Rural Improvements Calculated for Landscape and Picturesque Effects* (1797). He included a ruined monastic Gothic fold yard for sheep, and a cattle shed in three styles: Gothic, Classical or grotesque.

## FARM BUILDINGS
Farming was key to the management of parks and their appearance, with pasture for sheep, cattle and horses, dotted with scattered park trees and surrounded by tree belts for shade and shelter. These animals needed housing, which provided an ideal opportunity for ornamented buildings, and the most impressive farm buildings were for large livestock. Cattle did well for ornamental buildings: Exton Park, Leicestershire, has a pinnacled octagonal Gothic dovecote with an arcaded cowshed around five sides above the lake, probably of the late eighteenth century. Even more magnificently, at Burn Hall, County Durham, Sir John Soane in 1783 designed a cow house whose central pavilion had curved arcades linking to the lower pavilions with pyramidal roofs. Cow stalls ran along the length of the wings with central calf stalls, a bull pen behind, and the pavilions for hay lofts.

Cannon Hall Deer House, South Yorkshire, is a rustic and Gothic shelter of the early to mid-nineteenth century. The central five bays are open and the roof is supported by four yew trunks.

The Duchess's Dairy, Endsleigh, Devon, the country retreat of the dukes of Bedford, stands in the picturesque combe landscaped by Humphry Repton in 1814.

The interior of the Duchess's Dairy is lavishly fitted with Devon marble tables with channels for cooling water.

Badminton Park, Gloucestershire, has the very muscular Castle Barn with cow house, dovecotes in the towers and a central barn, in military Gothic style. This, with the nearby pigsty and stable at Swangrove House, was by Thomas Wright, belying his whimsical pattern book confections. The palatial Deer House at Bishop Auckland, County Durham was built for the Episcopal palace on an eminence in the deer park. It is arcaded, crenellated and pinnacled like a great cloister with a tower from which to watch the deer in the courtyard below in the rolling park. Constructed by Bishop Trevor in 1760, it was described in the mid-nineteenth century as being upon a graceful elevation above the River Gaunless, beneath the walls of the castle.

Dairies were the most feminine Georgian garden buildings, where in cool surroundings milkmaids separated the milk for cream and butter. Elegantly ornamented inside as well as out, they echoed Marie Antoinette playing at milk-maiding at Le Petit Trianon, Versailles. The dairy at Carton, County Kildare (*c.* 1770), has blue-and-white tiles and marble, its exterior in Classical style. By contrast, at Woburn the Chinese Dairy by Henry Holland (*c.* 1790s) in Chinoiserie style overlooks an ornamental pond in the pleasure ground. Prince Puckler in 1826 noted that it was decorated with 'a profusion of white marble and coloured glasses', with 'hundreds of large dishes and bowls of Chinese and Japanese porcelain of every form and colour filled with new milk and cream' lining the walls, and the room was cooled by a central fountain. For the 6th Duke of Bedford,

at his picturesque retreat at Endsleigh, Devon in 1816, Sir Jeffry Wyatville designed a two-storey dairy set into a hillside overlooking the pleasure ground and River Tamar; the upper room contained the dairy, lined with tiles.

The colourful Chinese Dairy at Woburn Abbey, in exuberant Chinoiserie style, with its ornamental pond. (Henry Holland, c. 1790s).

## SPORTING BUILDINGS

Landscape parks were intended for sport, and were ideal for hunting, shooting and fishing. Many contained sporting buildings for the animals involved. Again many were Gothic in style, including the 1760s kennels at

The Kennels at Milton Park, Cambridgeshire, were built for the Fitzwilliam Hunt as a ruined castle gatehouse, c. 1767.

23

Nunwick, Northumberland, those for the Fitzwilliam Hunt at Milton Park, Cambridgeshire of *c.* 1767 built as a ruined castle gatehouse, and at Castle Hill, Devon, where the remains of Earl Clinton's early eighteenth-century kennels survive, about 350 metres west of the house.

One of the most unusual uses for a Georgian garden building is the mid-eighteenth-century Netherby Salmon Coops, originally the keeper's house for the salmon coops for Netherby Hall, near Carlisle, Cumbria, as well as a park ornament and perhaps a summerhouse. Another 'castle' standing close to the Scots border, and now a Landmark Trust holiday let, it overlooks the river Esk and was built at the end of a stone weir, in front of which coops or traps were set to catch salmon. This annoyed the Scots upstream so much that, deprived of their salmon catch, they marched on Netherby in force, a scene described by Sir Walter Scott in *Redgauntlet*.

Sir Francis Dashwood's Arch of Apollo at West Wycombe, Buckinghamshire, was a muscular triumphal arch with a cockpit in its roof.

## PETS AND MENAGERIES

Buildings for pets and wild animals in parks and gardens included aviaries and menageries. They continued a long tradition of such buildings in parks, for the first menagerie in Britain was at Woodstock Palace (now Blenheim Park) in the twelfth century for Henry I, with lions, lynxes, leopards, camels and a porcupine. Again, the Gothic style was popular. The Peacock House at Hawkstone, Shropshire, looks more like an orangery; here the menagerie had birds and monkeys. Humphry Repton's aviary design (1808) for the Prince Regent's Indian tour de force at Brighton Pavilion was vaguely Eastern in style but rather odd in form.

Two neoclassical menageries in Northamptonshire were of extraordinary quality. The one at Castle Ashby (1760s) is in three sections, its central dome crowned by a dragon bearing an armorial shield. It may be by Lancelot 'Capability' Brown but it is more likely to have been designed by Robert Adam. At Horton Lord Halifax kept his private zoo surrounded by a moat, at the heart of which was an outstanding folly built in the 1750s by Thomas

Above: At the Netherby Salmon Coops the coops, or traps, set below this keeper's house annoyed the Scots upstream so much that, deprived of their salmon catch, they marched on Netherby in force, a scene described by Sir Walter Scott in *Redgauntlet*.

Opposite top left: The Bird House, Knole, Sevenoaks, Kent, *c.* 1761, was built to house exotic birds, doves and poultry, in a very engaging octagonal *cottage ornée* in the deer park, standing near purpose-built Gothic ruins.

Wright of Durham. Single storey, it has a long, imposing façade, which was both banqueting house and eyecatcher for Horton House (demolished), with the menagerie behind. It stood in a circular enclosure just over 2 acres in extent, described as 'a little wood, prettily disposed with many basons of gold fish'. Four of those circular ponds survive. The interior decoration was as important as the exterior and has fine plasterwork: on the ceiling is Father Time with scythe and symbol of Eternity; the Four Winds are depicted in the four corners; Apollo's head appears in a sunburst on the bay ceiling; and acanthus scrolls and cornucopias abound.

Above: The aviary designed by Humphry Repton for the Prince Regent at Brighton Pavilion.

Horton Menagerie, Northamptonshire, was both banqueting house and eyecatcher for Horton House (now demolished), with the animals housed to the rear, in a circular enclosure of 2 acres.

# BRIDGES AND CASCADES

WATER was the most prestigious feature in the landscape park: the larger and more natural-looking the lake or river, the better the Georgian owner was satisfied. Most areas of Britain were not blessed with naturally impressive water bodies or noisy, rocky cascades; technically it was difficult to achieve extensive sheets of water artificially and thus expensive to manipulate water. So there was great cachet involved if a large and natural-looking lake or river could be achieved within the park or garden, as Brown and his contemporaries usually could manage (although there were some notable disasters of engineering and occasionally there was just not enough water available).

## BRIDGES

Bridges were linking devices in the landscape, carrying people or their vehicles on paths and drives across water, at the same time showing off the water in the landscape to best advantage. Rugged naturalistic cascades ornamented the functional, and sometimes extensive, dams holding back the sheet of water, such as the Duke of Cumberland's very early example at Virginia Water, Surrey (1750s), and Brown's at Blenheim, Oxfordshire (1760s). Sometimes, instead of a cascade, a dam was ornamented by a sham bridge disguising an essential change in level between two lakes or pools, such as Kent's 1730s sham bridges at the sister landscapes of Stowe and Wotton Underwood, Buckinghamshire. Kent used similar façades for the cascades at Rousham around the same time.

The Shell Bridge, Stowe (William Kent, 1730s), divides the upper Alder river from the lower Worthies river and is planted with evergreen shrubs to disguise the join.

The stone-faced Five-arch Bridge at Wotton Underwood, Buckinghamshire (c. 1750s) disguises a dam with an overflow from a canal into a lake. It is similar to Kent's Shell Bridge at Stowe.

A bridge might also carry a drive over a path or public road, linking two parts of an estate; Brown's Dry Arch Bridge (1760s) at Croome Court, Worcestershire, carries one of the main drives across a tranquil pleasure ground walk to the lake, and is ornamented with fine Coade stone plaques of river gods on the key stones. This sort of bridge carrying a drive over a pleasure ground path was used elsewhere including at Painshill, Surrey, where one in the 'Roman' style linked the house and pleasure grounds.

Bridges were often Classical in style, built of dressed stone, with one or more arches, and cutwaters to push the water away from the masonry at the water level. These abounded in various sizes by all the best architects including Robert Adam, Lancelot Brown, James Paine and designers noted specifically for the construction of bridges such as Robert Mylne (designer of the first Blackfriars Bridge in London), and John Rennie (designer of

The Lower Cascade in Venus' Vale, Rousham (William Kent, 1730s). The façade is similar to his sham bridges at Stowe and Wotton Underwood.

the old Waterloo Bridge, London). The bridge at Compton Verney, Warwickshire, with its guardian sphinxes is variously attributed to Adam or Brown, while James Paine's triple-arched bridge at Chatsworth, Derbyshire, forms an essential element to the main approach to the house. Robert Mylne's slightly later Leafield Bridge in the Castle Park, Warwick, soars above the River Avon in a daring single span, and also has decorative Coade stone keystones. John Rennie built a

long, level bridge over Virginia Water, Surrey (1805), but perhaps his most ornamental bridge carried a drive at Stoneleigh Abbey, Warwickshire (1812–14).

Bridges often provided important points from which to view the landscape design, as well as providing visual interest and punctuation in views from elsewhere within the landscape. The grandest, and rarest because of the expense, were covered Palladian bridges, inspired by designs by the Italian architect Palladio published in 1570, himself using Roman models. The first of three of these was at Wilton House, Wiltshire (1737) by Roger Morris for Henry, 9th Earl of Pembroke, followed by a near replica at Stowe, Buckinghamshire (1740), for Lord Cobham, then an even larger one

Opposite:
The Palladian Bridge at Stowe (1740).

Vanbrugh's Great Bridge at Blenheim Palace, Oxfordshire, was partly submerged in the 1760s when 'Capability' Brown floated his sublime lake.

The restored Chinese Bridge at Painshill, Surrey, is a simple timber structure, evoking the Orient with its criss-cross parapet.

terminating the vista at the bottom of the valley at Prior Park, Bath (1765) for Ralph Allen. At Scampston Hall in North Yorkshire a more modest version with a painted timber superstructure was built (*c.* 1773) by Brown or his son-in-law Henry Holland; and there is another by Robert Adam (1783) spanning the River Cam at Audley End, Essex, now known as the Tea House Bridge.

Perhaps the acme of landscape bridges was Vanbrugh's early Grand Bridge (1710) over the River Glyme at Blenheim Park, Oxfordshire. It was intended to be covered, with towers and arcades rising to 25 metres high above the thirty-three rooms within it, and a main arch spanning 32 metres, but it never acquired the superstructure. However, it provided the massive scale that Brown required some fifty years later for his huge lake, and even though the lower floors were as a result flooded, the visitor still stands way above the water level to marvel at the sheer bulk.

While stone bridges were an expensive status-symbol, even owners with more modest means could aspire to timber bridges to ornament their landscapes (thus they were more ephemeral by design than masonry bridges). Timber bridges of a loosely 'Chinese' style were built at Painshill, Stowe, Wotton Underwood (all recently rebuilt) and Stourhead (now gone). The design could be varied by the steepness of the curve of the bridge itself, or through the use of decorative balustrades.

## CASCADES

Georgian cascades were generally picturesque and naturalistic rather than formal as they had been in the seventeenth century. They emulated the dramatic and noisy rocky rapids in rivers of the far west and north of the kingdom. The easiest and most effective method of achieving this was to graft a layer of ragged rock onto the outer side of a dam below the spillway; even if it was not seen it made a dramatic noise, heralding the exciting feature and drawing the visitor on. William Wrighte published a lively design in 1767 (see overleaf) and West Wycombe had something similar in the 1750s. One of the earliest and most dramatic of this sort was the cascade at Virginia Water, Surrey.

The picturesque cascade and grotto at Bowood is spectacular and very noisy. The extensive rock-work was added to the head of Brown's lake, with advice from Charles Hamilton of Painshill.

The rocky cascade at Virginia Water, rebuilt in the late eighteenth century.

William Wrighte's lively cascade design, published in 1767.

The cascade at West Wycombe Park in its original form (1750s), with a rocky superstructure, and a river god reclining in the torrent of water from the lake.

It was first constructed in the 1750s on the dam of what was then the largest artificial lake in England. It collapsed later in the century and was reconstructed by Thomas Sandby.

Cascades relied on good engineering to ensure an adequate supply of water, usually via systems of leats and conduits to convey the water to the

desired point, or sometimes with a pump, as at Chiswick in the 1730s. In the early 1760s, Coplestone Warre Bampfylde constructed at Hestercombe, Somerset, a 'Grand Cascade' in the valley behind the house, fed by a long, brick-lined leat. Somewhat later, Humphry Repton employed a similar system of leats along the sides of a steep valley to create a series of rocky cascades in the pleasure grounds at Endsleigh, Devon.

The manipulation of natural streams into chains of pools separated by dams and cascades offered some surprising opportunities for architectural embellishment. One of the most unusual examples is to be found at Halswell, Somerset, where in 1755 Thomas Wright, the so-called 'Wizard of Durham', designed a combined sham bridge and cascade for Sir Charles Tynte. Viewed from upstream the structure appears to be a bridge with a central recessed niche ornamented with lavish frost-work and vermiculation, and flanked by a pair of curious female figures; viewed from downstream, the structure appears to be a rocky cascade.

The sham bridge and cascade at Halswell, Somerset.

# CASTLES AND FORTS

SHAM CASTLES were hugely popular in Georgian gardens and parks where there was no real castle. They could be put up quickly and inexpensively as a theatrical feature in the park scenery, or be a major structure. Sometimes whole groups of park fortifications were built. Fortifications made a

Castle Howard, North Yorkshire, the first large-scale sham castle for a park (Sir John Vanbrugh, 1719).

statement of power and presence which was particularly valued by garden owners. This section deals with 'proper' castles, meaning more than just Gothic prospect towers, having myriad permutations of curtain walls, towers and battlements, built to appear complete, not ruined.

Vanbrugh again led the way, this time in fortified ornamental buildings. His Belvedere at Claremont, Surrey (*c.* 1716), dominated a slope above the mansion and a grass walk leading down in the opposite direction. In 1719, on the approach through the park to Castle Howard, Yorkshire, he built eleven towers on a monumental scale, linked by a massive curtain wall, being the first large-scale sham castle in England. It could almost be taken for a medieval town wall – indeed Vanbrugh had seen the town walls of Chester while considering this project. Vanbrugh's artificial fortifications influenced many other fortified farms, cottages, towers and screens.

A rash of sham castles developed after the 1720s, copying the character of the many surviving genuine examples. Search English Heritage's *Images of*

The Castle, Sledmere, Yorkshire (John Carr, 1778), was both a farmhouse and gateway.

Above:
Radway Tower,
Warwickshire, is
one of the earliest
sham castles, built
as a gate lodge by
Sanderson Miller
(1745–7), and
evoking, as Horace
Walpole put it,
'the true rust of
the Barons' Wars',

Above right:
The Gothic Tower,
Hartwell House,
(probably James
Gibbs, 1720s–30s)
is a little drum
tower nestled in
the Wilderness,
intended to evoke
Saxon origins.

*England* website for 'folly' as a building type and it throws up dozens of mock castles and turrets. Most were built of stone to emulate medieval fortifications, but occasionally they were of brick (such as Sledmere Castle Farm, Yorkshire, designed by John Carr). Fortifications were an easy and relatively cheap way to ornament a utilitarian estate building fashionably and to put the patina of age and patrician ownership on even a newly laid-out park. They were used all over the park and garden as eyecatchers and at entrances, but especially where they could be seen as a looming presence on high ground or from a distance. Radway Tower, on Edge Hill in Warwickshire, was designed *c.* 1746–7 by Sanderson Miller for his Radway Grange property, the first of a string of park castles he designed, often as ruins, over the next three decades. It was built as a prominent five-storey octagonal tower, within ruins, an upper room decorated with delicate Gothic plasterwork. Miller took as his pattern the genuinely medieval Guy's Tower at nearby Warwick Castle.

Many sham castles were summerhouses at distant points of the park, a destination for an excursion. Stainborough Castle (1728–30) was built in Wentworth Castle Park for Thomas Wentworth, 1st Earl of Strafford. It was an early and imposing example after Vanbrugh's Castle Howard towers and curtain wall, and Lord Bathurst's Alfred's Hall (1721) in Cirencester (built as a ruin; *see* Ruins).

Sham castles or mock forts were especially popular in more remote upland parts of Britain where they made a picturesque composition in the rugged landscape, both within and beyond parks, particularly in Cheshire, Cornwall, Devon, Cumbria, Lancashire and Wales. In the naturally picturesque Lake District, castles were built which could hardly be told apart from nearby genuine counterparts. Lyulph's Tower on Ullswater (1780s) is a hunting lodge in its own deer park, and Claife Station on Windermere (1790s) is a viewing pavilion, remodelled in the 1800s as a tiny castle with a tower and curtain wall overlooking the cylindrical Classical Belle Isle house.

Forts and castles had a variety of other uses. In Lancashire the dog kennels at Gisburne Park were built in the late eighteenth century as a sham castle by the River Ribble. Two round towers flank a lower central section in front of brick vaults.

Forts were ideal for *naumachia* (mock naval battles), most spectacularly at Newstead Park, Nottinghamshire, with two lake-side groups. Here the 5th Lord Byron built the Cannon Fort and adjoining dock (*c.* 1750) with triangular bastions at each end and curved steps. Each bastion has a circular tower with an adjoining dock. Visible across the lake, it formed a mooring for the ship kept for entertaining his friends with mock naval battles. Some years later (*c.* 1770) he built a second mock fort comprising The Fort, Fort Lodge and Monk's Laundry.

Newstead Abbey, Nottinghamshire. One of two lake-side forts, this one was built in about 1750 for mock naval battles.

Sham castles or forts were, as well as eyecatchers, often agricultural buildings or dwellings. Stowe Castle, Buckinghamshire (*c.* 1740, Gibbs) appeared from the garden and park as a vast fortified wall with arrow loops, battlements and corner towers, but screened a very modest farmhouse. Clytha Castle, Monmouthshire (1790) was a retreat and picnic house. The Folly in Raby Park, County Durham (1780, J. Carr) re-used the medieval barbican arch and other fragments from Raby Castle. Raby Home Farm (mid-eighteenth century, J. Paine) stood within a fortified screen incorporating medieval masonry, with a carved bull emblem from the demolished barbican of Raby Castle. Greystoke Castle, Cumbria, has a group of fortified agricultural buildings and farmhouses built *c.* 1780 by the 11th Duke of Norfolk. Two commemorate American independence: Fort Putnam is a farmhouse and outbuildings within a system of fortifications including the outside wall of the cow house, with a watch tower; Bunker's Hill farm is a simpler group. The great axial vista at Castle Hill, Devon, is terminated by the sham castle which was built by Hugh Fortescue, 1st Earl Clinton, on the hill top above the house (*c.* 1730). The castle, which was originally roofed and contained a furnished panelled room, stands on a bastion complete with saluting cannons.

Stowe Castle (*c.* 1740). James Gibbs's monumental curtain wall (it hid a small farmhouse) was one of a group, with the circular Bourbon Tower and triangular Gothic Temple as a 'medieval' trio.

Castle Barn, Badminton (Thomas Wright, 1748), is a great castellated barn with screen walls and towers.

The Sham Castle terminates the great axial vista at Castle Hill, Devon, built by the 1st Earl Clinton on the hilltop above the house (c. 1730). It was roofed, with a furnished panelled room, on a bastion complete with saluting cannons.

Clytha Castle, Monmouthshire, was erected in 1790 and stands as an eye-catcher, retreat and picnic house on the summit of a small hill.

# CHURCHES AND CHAPELS

CHURCHES had a prominent visual role in Georgian landscape gardens and parks, as a key feature in park and garden design or as part of the iconography; the churchyards that were incorporated into the park were often planted with trees as elements of the landscape design.

In some notable cases churches were rebuilt as park eyecatchers at the expense of the landowner. Such a church became a great declaration of the owner's taste, imagination and financial status, and sometimes (but not always) his religious devotion. At a time of great social and land reform during the Georgian period, it was sometimes possible for the wealthiest landowners to remove a village to another site out of view of the mansion and its landscape. It was an opportunity not just to provide a model village but also to create in the rebuilt church a great architectural statement standing in splendid isolation from most of the parishioners. At Croome Court, Worcestershire, and Nuneham Courtenay, Oxfordshire, the villages and their inhabitants were moved to the periphery of the newly extended park. At each the church was rebuilt on a new, prominent site in the park or garden which suited the landowner and the requirements of his landscape design more than the parishioners, who now lived at some inconvenient distance.

These two were early examples of parish churches re-built as garden ornaments. Both were constructed at the top of a slope dominating the grounds from many points below, visible beyond the park for miles around, and seen from the mansion. Naturally the best designers and craftsmen were employed. Brown's church at Croome

Lancelot Brown's church at Croome Court (1758) stands prominently above the mansion, informal lake and pleasure grounds, of which it has a great sweeping view across the park.

for the 6th Earl of Coventry (1758) was in Georgian Gothic with a prominent tower, its light and airy interior by Adam. At Nuneham the 1st Earl Harcourt's Classical landscape was laid out to offset his 1764 church built in the form of a Greek cross 'temple' with a central dome. As an amateur architect, Harcourt was advised by the professional James 'Athenian' Stuart who was an early expert on Greek architecture.

West Wycombe and Hartwell churches, Buckinghamshire, were even earlier examples, rebuilt in the mid-eighteenth century as garden eyecatchers in exceptional landscape designs. The medieval West Wycombe church, standing on top of the hill above the village and pleasure grounds, was remodelled as a Classical box in the later 1750s (see overleaf). The tower was earlier heightened and ornamented with a great wooden ball, gilded to terminate the view in the approach from High Wycombe constructed at the same time (now the A40). The ball could also seat ten men. It was the crowning glory of the ensemble rising up the hill above the pleasure ground, including the Gothic entrance to the Caves, and the huge Classical 1760s mausoleum below the church.

The 1760s church at Nuneham Courtenay was sited in the midst of the pleasure grounds overlooking the Thames and the distant 'dreaming spires' of Oxford, evoking an Arcadian scene by Claude or Poussin.

When the church at West Wycombe, Buckinghamshire, was remodelled in the 1750s in classical style, it was surmounted by a unique golden ball which shone out over the park and Chiltern landscape.

Henry Keene's 1750s Gothick church at Hartwell House was less prominent than some others, but it dominated the pleasure grounds on a rise in front of the mansion.

Hartwell church was built from scratch on a new site close to the old one, in 1752–3. It was more evidently a garden building than a place of worship, in whimsical Gothic style by architect Henry Keene, who was, appropriately enough, Surveyor to the Fabric of Westminster Abbey. It overlooked the house, at the heart of the garden. The churchyard was left on the other side of the lane; the real world was not allowed to intrude on the Arcadian landscaping scheme.

At Ayot St Lawrence, Hertfordshire, Lionel Lyde employed Nicholas Revett in 1778–9 to build a new church in the neoclassical style. This was another example of the Greek Revival, on the boundary of the park, with the main front as a landscape feature, facing Ayot House across the park. It was a complex composition, with the church portico flanked by screens leading to small open pavilions containing urns. Not to miss an opportunity, having dismantled the medieval parish church of St Lawrence, Lyde left the latter as a picturesque ruin.

Chapels built specifically for the family's use were also designed to ornament the scene. One of the most engaging is Horace Walpole's tiny 'Chapel in the Wood' at Strawberry Hill, in Twickenham, Middlesex. Designed by

Ayot St Lawrence church (1778–9), with its unusual screen and flanking pavilions, forms an eye-catcher from the mansion on the edge of the park.

Gayfere, the master mason at Westminster Abbey, and built 1772–4 to display Walpole's stained glass collection, it was his only stone building here. For greater authenticity the Portland stone façade was based on the tomb of Bishop Audley in Salisbury Cathedral.

There was no distinction between park chapels and churches in terms of size and style. The private neoclassical Chapel (James Paine, 1760–9) in the extensive pleasure ground at Gibside, Tyne and Wear,

Above: A design for a rustic chapel (Phelps, c. 1750s), possibly created for Hatch Court, Somerset, in an unusual rustic style echoing Hoare's so-called convent at Stourhead.

The Chapel in the Wood at Strawberry Hill was built well away from the house, tucked away on Walpole's serpentine 'sweet walk' through the pleasure ground.

magnificently terminates a long imposing grassy avenue called the Grand Walk (late 1740s). It is a perfect example of Georgian ecclesiastical architecture in the most select Classical style, and could equally well be a parish church.

In addition to genuine places of worship, Georgian landowners embellished their estates with ornamental buildings which derived their appearance from religious structures. Some, such as 'The Convent', set deep in the woods above Stourhead (early 1760s), or the slightly earlier chapel on a bastion in the wooded pleasure grounds at Hatch Court, Somerset, formed picturesque dwellings for staff, or retreats for the family within the wider landscape. Ornamental details such as Gothic windows, turrets and finials evoked an appropriately ecclesiastical air, while the use of thatch rendered them even more picturesque. They were never intended for worship, but were dedicated to pleasure and good living.

Other buildings, particularly those conceived as ecclesiastical ruins, used genuine fragments of medieval churches. The owner of Cranbury Park, Hampshire, acquired substantial fragments of medieval Netley Abbey outside Southampton, which he re-erected on the edge of the park as an eyecatcher from the house. A small house based on a pseudo-medieval church tower was attached behind the medieval stones.

The owner of Cranbury Park, Hampshire, acquired substantial fragments from the medieval Netley Abbey near Southampton in around 1770 and erected them on the edge of his park with a cottage adjoined.

# COLUMNS

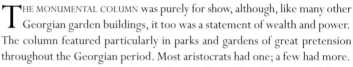

Trajan's Column, in
the Roman Forum,
is the most famous
antique column,
and the most
copied in Georgian
gardens.

T HE MONUMENTAL COLUMN was purely for show, although, like many other
Georgian garden buildings, it too was a statement of wealth and power.
The column featured particularly in parks and gardens of great pretension
throughout the Georgian period. Most aristocrats had one; a few had more.

The appeal came largely from the Roman model: to
commemorate a great man and to raise him above mortality.
Most Roman columns were built in the second century AD
to commemorate famous military and naval victories and to
exalt the emperor who presided over them. The most famous
column, and most copied in Georgian gardens, is that of
Trajan, a 35-metre-high Doric column with a relief sculpture
spiralling up its shaft depicting his victories, completed in
AD 113. A column dominating the scenery also declared the
familiarity of the owner with the Classical world.

The column was a true folly: a building without practical
use, although in some cases it was also a prospect tower for
the owner. Popularity with the wealthiest owners arose from
the sheer expense and obvious lack of function except as an
eyecatcher and spectacular viewing platform, which marked
it out as the preserve of only the wealthiest. Most other sorts
of garden buildings had a purpose beyond ornament, but, as
with the obelisk to which it was closely related in the garden,
there was little way of making the column functional (except
at the Desert de Retz in France where a broken column was
built of such diameter that it had rooms in it). The novelist E.
M. Forster summed it up when he wrote, 'Architecture has
evolved nothing more absurd than the monumental column.'

Wherever the column was sited (in town, garden or
park), above all it was designed to be ostentatious. The
contrast between the sophistication of the structure and its
associations, and the natural surroundings (however

contrived) was startling. As an eyecatcher, it stood prominently in the garden, park or wider landscape, and preferably enjoyed views of as many counties as possible from the top. At Hawkstone, Shropshire, the 30-metre-high column, erected in 1795 on the highest point on the estate, was surmounted by a statue of the owner, Sir Rowland Hill; it was said that from there thirteen counties could be seen. At Ashridge, Hertfordshire, the 40-metre-high Doric column (1831–2) is topped by a huge copper urn, above the viewing platform which forms the abacus, a flat slab on top of the capital. Commemorating Francis, 3rd Duke of Bridgewater, known as the 'Canal Duke', in one direction from the top of the Chiltern scarp it overlooks the Vale of Aylesbury and in the other Wyatt's great Gothic mansion along the seventeenth-century Princes Riding.

Below left: The Column of Liberty, at Gibside, County Durham (Daniel Garrett and James Paine, 1750s).

Below right: The Bridgewater Monument, Ashridge (1831–2), at the edge of the Chiltern scarp slope.

Right:
The Doric
Column, Chiswick
(c. 1720s) stands
at the heart of the
formal *allées* of
Lord Burlington's
seminal garden,
and was later
surrounded by the
mid-nineteenth-
century circular
rose garden.

Far right: The
slender Doric
Column at
Hartwell House
(1720s–30s),
similar to the one
at Chiswick House
but here topped
not by Venus, but
by King William III,
representing
Liberty.

Opposite, bottom:
Lord Cobham's
Pillar at Stowe is
an octagonal Doric
column with
enormous flutes
and topped by his
statue. It is one of
'Capability'
Brown's early
creations,
influenced by
James Gibbs.

Some less muscular columns were only seen within the estate, such as the smaller, more graceful early eighteenth-century examples in the gardens at Chiswick House, Middlesex, and Hartwell House, Buckinghamshire. At some 7.5 metres high, the smaller scale fitted better with their more intimate settings, that at Hartwell topped by King William III as a symbol of Liberty, and at Chiswick supporting Venus, each figure on a projecting abacus.

Like the Roman original, the Georgian garden column was usually built of ashlar blocks, or rendered to emulate stone, and the most magnificent were over 30 metres high. A fluted or plain shaft stood on a plinth. Being near eye level, the plinth was the ideal place for an inscription of dedication or exhortation – sometimes lengthy, as at Blenheim Palace, Oxfordshire. To correct the illusion of concavity produced by a straight shaft, a trick called 'entasis' was used: adding a slight convex curve in the shaft. John Carr's Keppel's Column, at Wentworth Woodhouse in Yorkshire (1773–81), is a Tuscan column some 35 metres high with strangely bulging entasis, as if a mistake had been made in the design – resulting from repeated changes of design by the Marquess of Rockingham, for whom it was built. A rostral column such as Captain Grenville's Column at Stowe, Buckinghamshire, was a naval variation in the Roman manner with sculpted prows of ships projecting from the shaft.

At the top of the column the capital was usually surmounted by a statue, or other sculpture, or by a belvedere. For the pleasure of the brave, an iron-railed viewing platform (forming the abacus) sometimes projected precariously around the top (at Ashridge, Plas Newydd, and Hawkstone, for example). Although usually male, female statues were sometimes used, such as the Venus de Medici at Chiswick (Middlesex), Flora at Syon Park (Middlesex) or Queen Caroline, wife of George II, at Stowe. The 43-metre-high column at Gibside, County Durham (Daniel Garrett and James Paine, 1750s), had a gilded statue of Liberty dominating the Derwent Valley, an overt expression of the owner George Bowes's nationalist and Whig political sympathies.

The most prominent columns pushed above the tree tops in parks. One of the earliest and best known is Blenheim's early and huge Column of Victory (1727–30, Nicholas Hawksmoor) at the heart of Oxfordshire. This was erected after the Duke of Marlborough's death, true to its Roman model: to commemorate his military victories. The 40-metre-high fluted Doric column stands on the great windswept plateau in the park dominating a great geometric avenue (originally elm) with the Duke modelled in lead as Caesar, supported by Roman eagles. At Stowe, Lord Cobham, one of the revered Marlborough's generals, occupies a belvedere above Capability Brown's attempt at entasis (1747).

Above: The Column of Victory at Blenheim Palace, Oxfordshire, (Nicholas Hawksmoor, 1727–30) commemorates the Duke of Marlborough's military victories. It stands more than half a mile from the palace and is framed by a great formal avenue that strides into the distance.

# DRUIDIANA

**D**RUIDIANA evoked the primitive native British in Georgian gardens. It reminded the visitor of his ancient and unsophisticated but libertarian origins and ancestors and perhaps of a certain magic and wizardry. This primitive, supposedly native-British, style was used in garden structures mainly relating to Druid worship and dwellings.

During the eighteenth century an interest in antiquities was fostered mainly by scholarly clergymen who were the forefathers of present-day archaeologists. This interest in ancient sites, and structures, was spurred by a wish to explain and understand sites such as Stonehenge and Avebury. Antiquarian William Stukeley published a study of Avebury in 1744, writing that the temple was an image of the Druid's 'divine being' which 'could not fail of drawing down the blessings of divine providence upon that place and country, as it were, by sympathy and similitude.'

Many gardens had one form of Druidiana or another, preferably located in a gloomy grove of venerable gnarled oak, the seminal tree of Druid ritual. Oakly Park, Shropshire, had ancient trees called 'Druid Oaks'. Many a Druid's cave or hut (sometimes with a live or an artificial Druid) was erected, also stone circles (cromlechs) and dolmen (a megalithic tomb of standing stones supporting a flat cap), but entire gardens devoted to primitive or antiquarian features were not favoured.

The archaic native features lay within a larger frame of miscellaneous styles such as Chinoiserie, Gothic and Classical. The 1720s saw the first primitive garden structures, with Stukeley's 'green' Druid Temple (1728) in his own garden at Grantham,

Thomas Wright's design for an arbour with Druidic associations: a cromlech and menhir flank the entrance.

Lincolnshire, composed of trees rather than masonry, with an old apple tree covered in mistletoe (another key Druidic plant). Buildings and monuments quickly followed elsewhere.

The amateur designer Thomas Wright, the 'Wizard of Durham', had great interest in native British antiquity, visiting Avebury in the 1740s and drawing it. He published designs for garden buildings, including a fanciful druid's cell (1755, in *Universal Architecture Book I, Six Original designs of Arbours*), which was flanked by a menhir (standing stone) and cromlech to establish its historical association (although the cell was in Gothic style).

Druidiana was best if it seemed authentically ancient, but only a few lucky owners could boast genuinely indigenous remains. Tourists of the Picturesque landscapes and learned antiquarians were particularly difficult to fool as they also knew of plenty in Wales, the Peak District, the Lake District and Ireland which they had visited or read about in guide books.

If a genuine structure was unavailable on site, importing one was perfectly acceptable. General Conway in 1787, when he was Governor General of Jersey, imported a spectacular stone circle to a hillside in his Berkshire landscape park, Park Place (a fact still bitterly lamented by the Jersiaise). Thomas Sandby designed the Grotto at Virginia Water, Surrey, in *c.* 1780–90, using monolithic stones dug on nearby Bagshot Heath and 'supposed to have belonged to a Druid's Temple'. But if nothing genuinely Druidic was available, then artifice – the more primitive the better – was fine. Druidic style, merging into the rustic, was cheap and easy to produce, hence its popularity even in relatively modest gardens.

Druidic worship and burial were represented by stone circles and monolithic assemblages. They could be entirely genuine prehistoric remains (such as at Amesbury Abbey and Wilton, Wiltshire, and the dolmens at Plas Newydd, Anglesey). Or they might be historically bogus but proclaiming

Megalithic monument removed from Jersey for its Governor, General Conway, and re-erected at Park Place, Berkshire, in 1788.

historical provenance via their authentic appearance, for example at Derwent Isle (Cumbria), Stouthall (Gower), Swinton Park (Yorkshire) and Alton Towers (Staffordshire); or else genuinely antique stones removed from other sites (such as the circles at Park Place, and at Bicton, Devon).

Monoliths were moved from a nearby megalithic tomb at Tisbury to Wardour Castle, Wiltshire, in the 1790s by Josiah Lane, who erected the stones near a grotto. The bogus circles often emulated those English examples most well known in the eighteenth century, most likely Stonehenge, but perhaps other circles such as the Rollright Stones (Oxfordshire).

Dwellings were represented by estate and garden buildings which suggested Druidic associations by their name and use of rustic or primitive architectural styles to emulate Druid habitations. As nobody knew what an authentic Druid habitation looked like it left the field open to creativity. Wright designed 'an artificial Grotto of the Bramage Kind, suppos'd to be the Habitation of a Bramin or Druid' (*Designs of Grottoes*, 1758). With a bath in the rearmost of its three chambers, its rustic primitive stonework looked like a ruin in a mountainous setting. His 1756 Druid Temple at Halswell, Somerset, was a small gazebo of knobbly rustic timber, with Gothic arches and windows as depicted in the design on the front of his *Designs of Arbours*

The Druid Circle at Swinton Park, Ilton, Yorkshire (early nineteenth century), an outlier to Swinton Park set on the rugged moors by William Danby as a spectacularly convincing fake.

(1755). The Druid's Hutt, West Wycombe, Buckinghamshire, is a modest estate worker's cottage, a *cottage ornée*, as is Druid Lodge, Plas Newydd, Anglesey, whose name is the main evocation of the native association although two genuine dolmens stand nearby in the park. Even the Marquess of Anglesey's yacht was called *Druid*.

Druid inhabitants conferred further authenticity, although generally they were statues. Mrs Coade did a regular trade in artificial stone statues of a Druid (at Erddig, Clwyd, and The Vyne, Hampshire). Some statues, such as at Shugborough, Staffordshire, embellished or were the focus of garden buildings; others were displayed on plinths in dark pleasure grounds (Croome Court, Worcestershire). A 'real' Druid (at least a man dressed as such) at Hawkstone, Shropshire, in the 1790s made a great hit. One visitor, whilst contemplating in a small chapel there, saw 'a venerable figure, clothed in the stole of a Druid, slowly passing from a dark recess in the apartment, [which] crossed before us much more surprised at, and almost ashamed of, the very singular impression which our minds could be made to experience.'

Above: The imitation Stonehenge at Alton Towers, Staffordshire, early nineteenth century.

Far left: The ultimate in Druidiana – a genuine Druid. Mrs Coade's Druid statue is at Croome Court, Worcestershire, on the pleasure ground walk (he has lost his staff). Others were put in the gardens at Erdigg and Shugborough.

Left: The Cromlech, Plas Newydd, Anglesey, a genuine prehistoric burial structure incorporated into the park design to evoke Druidic associations.

THE CROMLECH, A DRUIDICAL MONUMENT.
*AT PLAS NEWYD IN NORTH WALES.*
A SEAT of the EARL of UXBRIDGE.

# GATES AND
# GATEWAYS

Fᴵᴿꜱᴛ ɪᴍᴘʀᴇꜱꜱɪᴏɴꜱ ᴍᴀᴛᴛᴇʀ and the park gateway was important as the introduction to the estate. Straddling the entrance to the main drive, it had to convey various ideas, setting the scene for what was to come and giving an impression of the owner's wealth, power and taste, as well as practically ensuring that only invited visitors entered and livestock could not escape from the park. The gateways at the entrances to the main drives would be the most spectacular, marked by one or a pair of lodges for the gatekeeper; those for lesser drives or between the park and the garden were usually more modest and without a lodge. The gateways to a particular park might be all of a similar architectural style, or of a variety of styles, particularly if they were built over a long period.

A typical major park gateway had a central double carriage gate of wrought iron, flanked by one or two pedestrian gates in similar style, supported by stone or brick piers, or rarely iron ones. The grandest were

The Oxford Gates, Stowe (William Kent, 1730s) were moved out to the new park entrance in around 1760.

set back from the road with either an elegant iron screen either side (Chirk Castle, and Syon House, Middlesex) allowing tantalising views of the park, or masonry wing walls (Woburn Abbey) blocking the view. At Chirk Castle the early eighteenth-century screen and gateway by the Davies brothers of Wrexham is a masterpiece of wrought ironwork, moved from the main front of the Castle to its present position in 1888.

At Woburn the main London Entrance to the Abbey (Holland and Repton, 1810–11) is imposing. The stone gateway has a tall central carriage arch flanked by smaller pedestrian arches with latticed iron gates, leading out to 50-metre curving, stone screen walls framing an extensive apron of lawn adjacent to the road.

The most imposing park gateways were based on Roman triumphal arches (*see* Arches), the most substantial of which also incorporated lodge accommodation, such as at Berrington Hall (Herefordshire), Garrendon Park (Leicestershire) and Fonthill (Wiltshire). Adam's London Gateway at Croome Court is a less muscular arch, with refined decoration.

The screen and gateway at Chirk Castle (early eighteenth-century), by the Davies brothers of Wrexham, is a masterpiece of wrought ironwork.

Less prominent gates were sometimes wooden, and often in the lesser entrances the piers were wooden too.

Entrances often reflected the style of the house they heralded. When Thomas Weld embellished his estate at Lulworth Castle, Dorset, in the late eighteenth century, he built several new lodges, all of a more or less martial

Fonthill gateway (mid-eighteenth century) straddles the public road across the park towards Alderman Beckford's now lost Fonthill Splendens mansion.

London Gateway, Croome Court (Robert Adam, 1760s).

character. The North or Triangular lodges are a pair of triangular-plan castellated buildings with circular corner turrets, echoing the design of the seventeenth-century Castle. Similarly, the 2nd Earl of Warwick built a new castellated entrance to the Castle as part of his improvements in 1796–7. This gave a delicious foretaste of the medieval treat awaiting the visitor, and led to a new gloomy drive, cut through rock and overshadowed with trees, which heightened the dramatic impact of the Castle once the final bend

was passed – an experience which would have delighted every reader of the popular Mrs Radcliffe's Gothic novels.

Dunster Castle, Somerset – Phelps's design for a ruined tower on Conygar Hill.

By the latter part of the eighteenth century, a greater range of architectural styles was employed for lodges and entrances. In his 'Red Book' for Stoneleigh Abbey, Warwickshire (1809), Repton proposed that the entrance from the Coventry road should be marked by timber-framed cottages, recalling the Henry VIII lodge he had proposed for Woburn in 1804; the Stoneleigh cottages were not built, and instead a more conventional pair of Classical lodges was erected.

The entrance lodge at Chilworth Manor, one of a pair of rustic *cottage ornée* lodges.

The *cottage ornée* could form a suitable sentinel at the estate entrance. At Endsleigh, Devon, Jeffry Wyatville marked the entrance to the Duke of Bedford's rural retreat with a stone and thatched cottage. Slightly earlier, the entrance to the much more modest Chilworth Manor outside Southampton was marked by a pair of circular, thatched lodges with rustic tree-trunks set into the walls. In Dorset this style of entrance lodge is found at several estates. Two of the best examples are at Gaunt's House, Hinton Martell (*c.* 1809), and the Round House Lodge, Charborough Park (*c.* 1810).

The garden gateway did not have to keep visitors (invited and uninvited) and livestock in their place. Thus it could be less muscular and more elegant, suitable to the ladies' realm. The Gothic gateway to the forecourt at Lacock House, Wiltshire, is a swooping stone ogee arch with a carved pinnacle, intended

The gateway to Mrs Johnes's Garden at Hafod, an enclosed flower garden in a great landscape park.

by the designer Sanderson Miller to evoke the medieval and Tudor origins of the mansion. A Classical style was used elsewhere, as at Rousham, Oxfordshire, for the large stone gateway for garden visitors who were not also guests of the family. This type of pedimented garden door had a long and honourable tradition in English gardens, stretching back to Inigo Jones's work in the 1630s.

Georgian walled gardens tended to be restricted to the kitchen garden (which might also include an area for growing flowers), with gateways integral to the walls. An exception is Mrs Johnes's Garden, Hafod, Ceredigion, where the slate gateway is ornamented with vermiculated stone and a fine key stone with a female mask. Freestanding gateways were less common in the garden.

Various styles were adopted, sometimes for reasons of apparently pure whimsy: at Prior Park, Bath, Ralph Allen's timber garden gateway from the public road into the pleasure ground is Chinese in style where his main garden features were Classical.

Visitor gate, Rousham (William Kent, 1730s). At some popular gardens, including Stowe, a gate was provided for visitors.

# GROTTOES

THE GROTTO was the most whimsical of garden buildings, but its clear aim on the garden circuit was to provoke great heights and depths of emotion. The essence of the grotto contrasted gloomy foreboding, pleasurable surprise and, with luck, a terrific sparkle never forgotten.

The concept of the grotto originated in Classical Greece and Rome as the shrine to the spirit of a spring, usually a nymph or river god. In the Georgian garden many were enthusiastically created with great imagination, and often expense. The interior was best found as a surprise, so the approach was artfully concealed in the pleasure ground in a natural hillside or behind banks of imported earth planted with evergreen shrubs, framing a dark and terrifying entrance. 'Grottish' and 'grotesque' described the desired effect.

Left: The monolithic entrance to a grotto at Fonthill.

Below: *A Rural Grotto* (1767), a design by William Wrighte, with a craggy façade of Classical conception, and Neptune at the centre, flanked by putti.

The frisson of the gloom had to be braved, often along a dark, twisting and turning tunnel made more scary (the fright heightened perhaps after reading a fashionable Gothic novel) by an uneven floor, before reaching whatever bright, decorative surprise awaited the intrepid visitor. It was important firstly to stir the imagination to fear the sublimely terrifying end to the dark and Gothic journey, but then for the resolute to encounter a great surprise at the watery, glittery and glistening cavern decorated to delight and enrapture in the exact opposite of the expected horror.

In desirable waterside situations such as at Stourhead, Somerset, and Stowe, Buckinghamshire, the cavern overlooked water through a rocky arch, a spring trickling through the rear wall into a pool and then into the lake or pond outside, the sound of running water heightening the emotions, and the play of sunlight on water making the whole chamber light up and sparkle. Fonthill, Wiltshire, has a unique group of lakeside grottoes with primitive monolithic exteriors, the caverns brought to life with the play of water glinting on the rock and mineral decoration of the walls and ceilings.

The Grotto at Stourhead is inhabited by the smooth and constantly soaked reclining nymph of the grot in the central chamber and her brooding river god in a side chamber, who gazes through craggy openings across the lake to the Palladian Bridge and Temple of Apollo.

The Grotto at Painshill, Surrey, overlooked the lake and was one of the most spectacular, with artificial stalactites sparkling with myriad slivers of applied quartz and mica.

Sometimes a so-called grotto was merely an alcove overlooking the water; it could be shell-shaped, or combine several alcoves, such as at Croome Court, Worcestershire, for the Earl of Coventry. Here, as at many other examples, a statue of the presiding river nymph was installed: the reclining Coade stone statue was said to be Sabrina, the nymph of the nearby River Severn. At Stowe a statue of the Crouching Venus presided, and at Stourhead a Classical reclining nymph was constantly wetted by the spring; in an adjacent cavern her bearded river god emerged from the water.

The most sophisticated grottoes had several entrances and passages, such as Stourhead (Wiltshire), Painshill (Surrey), Goldney House (Bristol), and Ascot Place (Berkshire). In this way the visitor left through another passage emerging at a different point, discombobulated with the sublime emotions. Simple grottoes might be a single room, or one with small side chambers such as at Prior Park (Bath) and Marlborough (Wiltshire). These did not have such a terrifying air, but this was made up for in the colourful and renowned complexity of decoration.

If the owner was lucky he had a slope into which the grotto was built, giving it a natural advantage of concealment and the possibility of tunnelling through the hillside to the main chamber. On flat ground the next best thing was to make a mound, possibly using spoil from the adjacent newly dug lake, and cover it with evergreens to make it blend into the rest of the garden, such as at Ascot Place, Berkshire. The structure was usually stone-lined to make it seem as natural as possible. Otherwise, as at Painshill, vaulting supported a wooden framework to shape plaster stalactites set with spar and other sparkling minerals. The use of the widest variety of stone for decoration revealed the owner's grasp of local and foreign geology, or their trading links with far-flung parts; sometimes grottoes were embellished with fossils such as ammonites. Sparkle and reflection of light was much sought after and provided by minerals and mirrors. At the poet Alexander Pope's grotto in Twickenham, Middlesex, and at his friend Ralph Allen's Prior Park, Bath (1740s), glittering minerals, stones and fossils from all over the world were acquired as trophies to display the wealth, knowledge and taste of the owners.

Above: Goldney House grotto, Bristol (1730s–60s). The interior is breathtaking in its colourful range of materials, including minerals and shells (both British and exotic), the imagination and skill with which they are used and its extent.

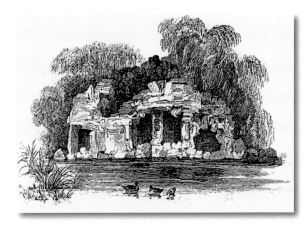

Previous page, bottom: Ascot Place's Grotto, Berkshire (possibly Thomas Sandby, *c.* 1790s) is cleverly disguised as a rocky outcrop in the otherwise flat park, with several chambers opening to the lake. Its interior decoration is another breathtaking *tour de force* of skill and artistry in applying shells and minerals of the quality of Goldney House.

Decoration was a personal thing and something in which the lady of the house was closely involved, as was Mrs Allen at Prior Park. Shell decoration was a popular pastime for wealthy ladies, with shells being imported from all over the world via their husbands' trade ships or brought back by enterprising merchants. The shell grotto at Goodwood is a formal room with exquisite shell-work, reputedly by the Duchess of Richmond. The subterranean shell grotto at Margate has tunnels and whole rooms embellished with local shells, limpets, sea urchins, mussels and others, punctuated by a few huge exotic conches, in complex and originally very colourful patterns.

Marlborough grotto, Wiltshire, has a plain brick exterior concealing the three exquisite chambers set into the great mount. Lady Hertford's decorations of the 1720s included 'ev'ry polish'd Stone', 'rustic Moss', 'the shining Pearl' and 'purple Shell' according to Stephen Duck in 1736.

# HERMITAGES AND ROOT HOUSES

I N GARDEN HERMITAGES dwelt solitary rustics, or at least that was the intended impression. The primitive form of the garden hermitage was similar to Druid cells (*see* Druidiana) and root houses. A root house was a very rustic building based on piles of root boles, with trunks, logs, moss and other vegetation for decoration. Unlike grottoes, rotundas and many other garden buildings, they had no real architectural precedent and flights of creativity were freely expressed in a primitive and irregular way. The hermitage was notionally intended as a dwelling but was generally simple and more like a summerhouse. Its setting was one of tranquil meditation and retreat, away from worldly goods and seductions, embowered in contemplative dark pleasure grounds or woodland planting of trees and shrubs.

Like the Druid's cell, an inhabitant was preferable, to confer the right ambience. A resident recluse could be hired in exchange for free accommodation (although the hermitage was often of insubstantial materials and not well appointed for long-term dwelling), food and modest wages but such individuals were not always committed to the secluded and ascetic life. An easier solution was to install a resident dummy got up to suit the part.

The form varied, but was usually a single room in rustic style, either of rough timber or masonry, often thatched to add an air of rusticity. William Wrighte's *Grotesque Architecture* (1767) had a range of hermitages in a choice of styles. Thomas Wright's *Universal Architecture* (Arbours, 1755) depicted timber and thatched pavilions which could be used for this purpose. The rustic Root

Merlin's Cave (William Kent, 1731), Richmond Gardens (now part of Kew Gardens), was built for Queen Caroline as a rustic retreat.

MERLIN'S CAVE

Above: Stowe's Hermitage overlooks the Eleven Acre Lake and is a rustic stone chamber with a bell turret (William Kent, c. 1731), almost identical to the one at Kew, now lost.

House at Spetchley, Worcestershire, is one such; with its conical thatched roof, four gnarled elm posts in front, and decorative panels of hazel withies inside, it is identical to Wright's arbour frontispiece with a wise owl on a nearby branch.

An early example was William Kent's ruined Classical Hermitage (1731) for Queen Caroline at Richmond (now part of Kew Gardens), built of rusticated stone. It had three rooms, a pediment over the main door and a small bell cote and was similar to the Hermitage he designed at Stowe.

Nearby, Kent's loosely Gothic Merlin's Cave (1735) for the queen was the precursor of rustic retreats, uniquely redolent of both hermits and Druidiana with extraordinary conical beehive-like thatched roofs reminiscent of Ancient British or Druidical houses seen in antiquarian illustrations. A central pavilion had small octagonal wings containing a library. The venerable look of the area which included the hermitage, Merlin's Cave, and its adjacent pond, was 'improved by the thickness of the solemn grove behind'. Six life-size wax-work figures were arranged in a tableau at the rear of the central chamber, including Merlin and Queen Elizabeth. The scene was loaded with

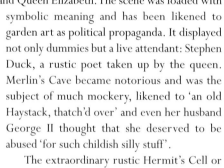

symbolic meaning and has been likened to garden art as political propaganda. It displayed not only dummies but a live attendant: Stephen Duck, a rustic poet taken up by the queen. Merlin's Cave became notorious and was the subject of much mockery, likened to 'an old Haystack, thatch'd over' and even her husband George II thought that she deserved to be abused 'for such childish silly stuff'.

The extraordinary rustic Hermit's Cell or Root House, Badminton, Gloucestershire, was built c. 1750 by Thomas Wright. It is the best surviving example, and remains a startling building. It was constructed in rustic style of wood with a thatched roof, with overhanging eaves and four large, knotty tree trunks at the corners; the walls are infilled with branches, roots and sawn timber. At the rear an inverted tree trunk fork shelters a rustic seat with an ogee back and an inscription in nailheads reads:

Opposite, bottom: The Hermitage, Painshill Park (recently rebuilt) is timber-framed and perches precariously above a valley at the farthest part of the pleasure ground as a little summerhouse with views over heathy Surrey.

'Here loungers loiter, here the weary rest'. Inside, arched niches are lined with bark and moss with a ribbed and panelled ceiling of timber with bark, moss and burr elm covering.

The Painshill Hermitage (recently rebuilt) was a more ephemeral affair, more like a tree house. Its crude timber-framed structure supported a thatched roof and lantern above, precariously supported above a hollow on large trunks and branches. The Gothic windows enjoyed an unexpected view over Surrey. The approach and surroundings were dark and gloomy as required for the contemplative life, but even so Hamilton had no success in retaining hermits. He apparently advertised for one under arduous terms of service, including no payment until seven years had elapsed. The hermit was to be silent, to remain in the grounds, and was given a Bible, a rush mat and an hourglass. The chosen incumbent lasted for three weeks before being discovered in the nearest hostelry.

The Hermitage at Brocklesby, Lincolnshire, was built around 1760 as a very primitive room.

Other notable hermitages were at Dunkeld, Scotland (mid-eighteenth century, with coloured glass, it stood above tumbling falls and was later called Ossian's Hall); Brocklesby, Lincolnshire (a small octagonal structure of rustic timber and tufa, *c.* 1760); Stourhead, Wiltshire (1771, dismantled 1814, built of old trees and masonry and lit by shafts of light, and

Right: At Hawkstone a resident Hermit made the thatched Hermitage (1780s) seem almost authentic to visitors.

Far right: The Temple of Vaccinia in the garden of Edward Jenner's home at Berkeley, Gloucestershire, where he vaccinated the poor of the area against smallpox for free.

also known as the Druid's Cell); Castle Hill, Devon (Earl Clinton's Hermitage); Hawkstone, Shropshire (thatched, 1780s); and Fonthill, Wiltshire (late eighteenth century, a primitive rocky cave with reliefs).

The decline of hermit mania was summed up by Horace Walpole:

> Men tire of expense that is obvious to few spectators … the ornament whose merit soonest fades, is the hermitage, or scene adapted to contemplation. It is almost comic to set aside a quarter of one's garden to be melancholy in.

The Hermitage at Fonthill, set into a park hillside, its large rocky cavern glittering with minerals and carvings in relief on the walls.

# MAUSOLEA
# AND MONUMENTS

MONUMENTS AND MAUSOLEA commemorated both people and, perhaps more surprisingly, animals. Today it may seem a strange idea to engender thoughts of mortality in a landscape of pleasure and Arcadian beauty rather than in a churchyard or other burial ground, but during the eighteenth-century Enlightenment it was a common theme, and one to which visitors readily responded.

Mausolea were intended to receive the remains of a former owner, perhaps the person who created the landscape, and his family. Most were enclosed buildings in Classical style on a park circuit route, so that they were not only a landscape incident but also a place for rest and contemplation, such as the Howard Mausoleum at Castle Howard, North Yorkshire, and the Darnley Mausoleum (1783, designed by James Wyatt) at Cobham Park, Kent. These two large Classical buildings were both intended to hold future generations and had generous provision for coffins in the crypt below a mortuary chapel, but at Cobham this facility was never used. Wyatt was also responsible for designing the circular Classical Mausoleum for Lord Yarborough at Brocklesby, Lincolnshire (1786–94).

At Castle Howard the sandstone Mausoleum stands on a high bastion on a knoll out in the park nearly a mile distant from the mansion. It is a closed rotunda (*see* Rotundas) with a vaulted crypt below, able to hold dozens of coffins. It was built in the 1730s to a design by Nicholas Hawksmoor for Charles Howard, 3rd Earl of Carlisle, who built the great mansion. Horace Walpole wrote of this fine building that it 'would tempt one to be buried alive'. The more austere Darnley Mausoleum is of Portland

The Darnley Mausoleum (James Wyatt, late eighteenth century), Cobham Park, Kent, has recently been restored after many years of dereliction.

stone, square and topped by a pyramid. To make the point it is embellished with tomb chests on the exterior. It has a circular chapel up several steps, with a plaster dome. Below, the basement held some thirty-two coffin shelves. The Yarborough Mausoleum is similarly decorated with reliefs of sarcophagi and bucrania (rams' skulls); even the railings protecting its enclosure in the park are supported by piers in the form of Classical sarcophagi. The vault below this mausoleum has, in contrast to that at Cobham, been used, the architect having even provided special small loculi for children's coffins.

During the eighteenth century, the vast majority of mausolea and monuments within landscapes were designed in a Classical style, reflecting the Georgian gentleman's familiarity with the Classical world and its commemoration of the dead, whether through his education, through artistic representations of Classical scenes or engravings of antiquities, or even through direct experience on the Grand Tour.

Many mausolea were visible from way beyond the park, such as the huge mausoleum at West Wycombe, Buckinghamshire. This was a five-sided open structure with a great archway in each of the three walls which had long views. It was visible not just from the distant mansion at the bottom of the hill but in the axial approach along the Oxford Road from High Wycombe some 2 miles distant, as well as from the Aylesbury road. While some were monumental, including the Seaton Delaval Hall Mausoleum, Northumberland (1776), with its dome and giant porticos, others were more modest.

Towards the end of the eighteenth century the Egyptian style became increasingly popular for mausolea, not least because it was understood that the ancient Egyptians held their dead in high regard. Pyramidal mausolea were constructed for Lord Luxborough at Barrels, Warwickshire (1792–4) and for the Earl of Buckinghamshire at Blickling, Norfolk (1794–6) to designs by Joseph Bonomi. The Luxborough Mausoleum was demolished in the early twentieth century.

People and animals were commemorated by monuments. Lancelot Brown has a column in the garden at Wrest Park, Bedfordshire (c. 1760) and a Coade stone casket on a pedestal at Croome Court (1797), commemorating his work at these places. The poet and elegist Thomas Gray, who grew up at Stoke Poges, Buckinghamshire, was commemorated in Stoke Park by its then owner, John Penn, grandson of William Penn (the American colonist). The monument (1799, designed by James Wyatt) was redolent of that of the eighteenth-century philosopher Rousseau in France. A large stone pedestal has panels inscribed with verses from Gray's *Elegy in a Country Churchyard* and is topped by a sarcophagus. At Stowe the dramatist Congreve was more playfully commemorated by a steep stone pyramid by William

Opposite:
The Mausoleum, Castle Howard (Hawksmoor and others 1729–40), is a closed rotunda on a great bastion which has always dominated the park and the garden.

Right: 'Capability' Brown's Monument, Wrest Park, Bedfordshire (c. 1760), in the pleasure ground, commemorates his work there for Jemima Grey.

Far right: Grey's Monument, Stoke Poges, stands in parkland close to where he lived and wrote his *Elegy*.

Below: The playwright and poet William Congreve's Monument, Stowe (William Kent, 1736), stands on Monkey Island, a playful monument commemorating a friend of Lord Cobham.

Congreve's Monument

Kent in 1736. It is embellished with a monkey at the top looking into a mirror, and a Latin inscription that tells us that comedy is the imitation of life and the mirror of fashion.

On a much grander scale, at Wentworth Woodhouse, South Yorkshire, John Carr of York built the enormous Rockingham Monument (1784–7) for William Wentworth Fitzwilliam in memory of his uncle, Charles Wentworth, 2nd Marquess of Rockingham and prime minister at the time of his death in 1782. The tall, tiered, three-stage sandstone monument is surrounded by four free-standing early eighteenth-century obelisks (moved by Repton from the garden west of the house) within a circular enclosure on the outskirts of the park. Carr derived the design for the Monument from the Tomb of the Julii at Glanum, the Roman town outside St Remy-en-Provence, France, which he almost certainly knew only through engravings. The Rockingham Monument is one of a group of great monuments conceived on an heroic scale which ring the park.

The Coade factory in Lambeth produced ornaments in its patent artificial stone which were ideal for use as monuments. George Holgate, a tenant farmer on Lord Yarborough's estate, Brocklesby, Lincolnshire, is commemorated in the gardens by a Coade stone monument, said to have been designed by James Wyatt in 1785. The distinctive design of this monument, with a triangular column supported on the backs of three

The Roman Tomb of the Julii at Glanum, near St Remy de Provence, France, on which John Carr based the Rockingham Monument at Wentworth Woodhouse (1784–7).

tortoises, is almost identical to another Coade stone monument at Mount Edgcumbe, Cornwall, commemorating Timothy Brett (1791), who had erected several of the buildings and follies on the estate. Nearby, a Coade stone urn commemorates Sophia, Countess of Mount Edgcumbe (1803).

Monuments to animals were also popular in the landscape scene, particularly pets and horses. In the garden at Shugborough, Staffordshire, is a swagged monument to a cat. The urn has the figure of a cat on its top, standing on a square plinth. The cat in question is probably the last of the Persian cats that Thomas Anson kept at Shugborough in the mid-eighteenth century.

Dogs, as pets, were much more commonly commemorated than cats. At Newstead Abbey, Nottinghamshire, Lord Byron, who surrounded himself with animals, erected a monument in the garden to the memory of Boatswain, his Newfoundland, which died of rabies in 1808. The square stone plinth, topped by an urn, stands on a circular flight of stone steps. Once again, the Coade factory provided artefacts suitable for use in commemorating much-loved dogs: Old Windham, a faithful dog belonging to Lord Yarborough, is commemorated at Brocklesby by a statue of a dog dated 1833; and at Wrest Park, Bedfordshire, a statue of a dog forms the focal point of a pets' cemetery in the garden.

Somewhat earlier, in 1765, Sir Charles Tynte of Halswell, Somerset, commemorated his favourite horse with a monument designed by Thomas Wright, who rather curiously decided to recycle the design of a monument he had built in 1756 at Stoke Park, Bristol, to commemorate the Duke of Beaufort.

A modest monument to a cat in the garden at Shugborough.

Pets' cemeteries seem to be a late eighteenth-century innovation, which increased in popularity during the following century. These features perhaps fitted well with the new taste for the picturesque. At Mount Edgcumbe a shallow quarry in the pleasure grounds was planted with ferns and furnished with fragments of Classical stonework as the burial place for the family's pets – one of the most unusual of which is said to have been Cupid the pig, who belonged to Emma, Countess of Mount Edgcumbe (d. 1807). There is some doubt as to whether this illustrious pig was laid to rest in the cemetery, or perhaps beneath an obelisk which was rebuilt at Cremyll at about the time of his death. Curiously, the crest of the Edgcumbe family is a boar.

# OBELISKS AND PYRAMIDS

OBELISKS AND PYRAMIDS have a similar simple form which can make it seem, incorrectly, that the broader pyramid developed from the narrow, needle-like obelisk. Instead they had different origins in ancient Egypt: obelisks as monuments inscribed with hieroglyphics, and pyramids as mausolea, and both were imported into ancient Roman culture once Rome had conquered Egypt.

The obelisk was not just imitated by the Romans: many were physically moved from Egypt and re-erected in Rome. Subsequently, during the Renaissance, many obelisks were re-utilised by successive Popes to serve as focal points in their rebuilding of Rome and these can still be seen all over the Eternal City. It was the *idea* of the pyramid that was imported to ancient Rome. As with other ancient structures, British Grand Tourists saw them in Italy, became familiar with their Classical context, allusions and origin, and considered them suitable models to copy and adapt to enliven the landscape garden and contribute Classical allusions. Egyptian elements were of particular importance in Georgian Freemasonry, and this symbolism helped to popularise their use in the landscapes of wealthy Freemasons.

The obelisk was relatively straightforward to design. Its simple, needle-like form meant that its sole function was as an eyecatcher in the landscape (although occasionally used as a landmark for shipping), or to commemorate a person or event. It proved that the owner had considerable wealth that could be spent on an otherwise useless ornamental feature to display his taste. Obelisks proliferated in Georgian parks and gardens, all in dressed stone and topped by a variety of finials including suns, urns and balls. The one at Kingston Lacy, Dorset, can boast authenticity: it is genuine Egyptian, from Philae in Upper Egypt, placed prominently in the garden in 1819 in line with the mansion.

Early in the Georgian period James Gibbs provided model obelisks when he published six similar designs for typical obelisks in his 1728 pattern book *A Book of Architecture* and explained how proportionally the height reflected up to eight times the width of the base. Some were topped by finials or urns;

all stood on squared plinths with panels for decorative sculpture, a device copied from the Italian architects in Baroque Rome who used them to enliven the otherwise rather austere ancient structures.

In Georgian gardens and parks, obelisks were sometimes isolated eyecatchers at the edge of the garden or park, such as the relatively modest, but slender example at Hall Barn, Buckinghamshire, on the perimeter of the garden, its pedestal embellished by fine sculptures in relief. Some marked the convergence of formal walks or rides, as does the large obelisk at Bramham Park, West Yorkshire (*c.* 1768, John Carr) marking a *rond point* where ten avenues meet in woodland and commemorating the son of the 2nd Lord Bingley; the one at Tring Park, Hertfordshire, some 15 metres high, was built

Right: Obelisk designs by James Gibbs, for use in gardens, 1728.

Far right: The obelisk, Tring Park, Hertfordshire (James Gibbs, 1720s), stands high in the woods in originally formal pleasure grounds, above the park and remote from the mansion.

in the 1720s by James Gibbs when Charles Bridgeman was laying out the park and pleasure grounds. It too marks a *rond point* where formal walks in the hanging Chiltern woodland meet at Gibbs's obelisk. A similar one arose below the Chiltern scarp at nearby Hartwell House, Buckinghamshire. Sometimes the obelisk marked a major axis, such as Lord Leicester's 25-metre high example at Holkham Hall (1729) on the southern axis of the mansion, marking the start of his great house-building and park landscaping campaign.

As tall structures, obelisks lend themselves as eyecatchers over a wide area. The obelisk at Farnborough Hall, Warwickshire, built by the Warwick mason William Hiorn for William Holbech by 1746, stands at the end of a terrace walk rising from the Hall to a high point overlooking a wide valley. Originally the walk continued to a Pentagonal Temple, now lost, but the obelisk remains visible for miles around (and has become a landmark from the M40 motorway). Similarly, the obelisk built in 1771 by the amateur architect Thomas Pitt, Lord Camelford (best known, perhaps, for his work for his cousin Earl Temple at Stowe) at Boconnoc, his own estate in Cornwall, is seen from a wide surrounding area.

Some obelisks within coastal designed landscapes are said to have served a dual purpose as ornament and navigational aids for shipping. The obelisk at Mamhead, Devon, was built by the Ball family in 1742 on a ridge of high ground above their park, overlooking the Exe estuary; the rather shorter obelisk which now stands at Cremyll overlooking the Hamoaze, on the Mount Edgcumbe estate in Cornwall, appears originally to have been built on higher ground overlooking Plymouth Sound (on a site now occupied by the Gothic Ruin of 1747), to serve as a day-mark to shipping.

The obelisk at Hartwell House (James Gibbs, 1720s–30s) was originally in a formal garden setting close to the mansion, above a pool.

Pyramids generally had a funereal association in the Georgian landscape, many being reminiscent of that of the first century AD for Caius Cestius in Rome (in turn based on Egyptian models), a square-plan structure seen by the Grand Tourists and much copied or adapted. Most Georgian examples are memorials or mausolea; many had Masonic associations. They also had associations with Whig concepts of Liberty, based on their Egyptian origins, along

The Needle's Eye, Wentworth Woodhouse (1722–3), through which a drive ran.

with Saxon towers and other structures. Pyramids were not as common as obelisks, probably because they were more expensive to build. However, illustrations of the Egyptian pyramids were published by J. B. Fischer von Erlach in the 1720s and were available to Georgian owners and designers.

One of the earliest pyramidal structures as a landscape feature is The Needle's Eye (1722–3) at Wentworth Woodhouse. Unusually, it was not a commemorative monument, but a point of interest on a drive to the house, visitors passing through the ogee arch in the pyramid. Although surmounted by an urn, this contains carved flowers and foliage rather than a flame of commemoration.

Another early and substantial example was constructed at Castle Howard, North Yorkshire, by Nicholas Hawksmoor, c. 1727–8, in memory of Lord William Howard (d. 1639) whose bust is within the beehive vault. Some 8 metres high and built of limestone, it stands on an axis with the south front of the mansion, on a rise in the park about 900 metres distant. Architect Sir John Vanbrugh had proposed one at Stowe in c. 1720 but it was not built until 1726 after his death, and dedicated to his memory. It stood on a stone plinth at the far edge of Lord Cobham's Western Garden, in a walnut grove on the circuit walk around the Home Park, but was taken down in the 1770s.

The Egyptian pyramid at Stowe, (c. 1726), stood in a walnut grove, prominently seen from the rest of the circuit around the Home Park.

The pyramid at Stanway, Gloucestershire, is a large and prominent structure, some 22 metres high. It was built in 1750 by Robert Tracy to commemorate his father and it stands at the heart of the formal pleasure ground, at the top of the former great cascade in front of a pool. It is more complex than many others as it stands on a cubed base of golden stone with four arches; this was intended as an ornate garden room with spectacular views beyond the

The pyramid at Hartwell (1720s–30s) was a diminutive version of the one at Stowe, and stood in a flowering shrubbery with the Gothic Tower.

The pyramid at Stanway (1750) is unusual as it stands on a base which itself was designed as a finely decorated summerhouse.

Cotswold countryside from its high vantage point over the Vale of Gloucester to the Malverns, and the Black Mountains of Wales. In contrast, the pyramid at Hartwell House, Buckinghamshire (c. 1730s) was a diminutive example –about 5 or 6 metres high – with stepped sides, as at Stowe. It stood in a gaily flowering shrubbery within an informal wilderness, but it has long gone.

Pyramids were built throughout the Georgian period. The one at Blickling Hall, Norfolk, is a late example, built as a mausoleum by Joseph Bonomi after the death in 1793 of John Hobart, 2nd Earl of Buckingham. Of limestone, it stands in Great Wood, about half a mile from the Hall, and is reached from the edge of the wood by a grass clearing bordered with great yew hedges. It is embellished by a coat of arms over the entrance supported by a stag and hound, and a bull set over the inscription at the rear. The form reprises Bonomi's slightly earlier mausoleum for Lord Luxborough at Barrels, Warwickshire (now gone).

# ORANGERIES AND CONSERVATORIES

The orangery
housing tender
plants at
Kensington Palace
(Wren, 1704)
had a great
influence on
ornamental
structures for
the rest of the
century.

G EORGIAN GARDEN HOTHOUSES developed with advances in technology;
they reflected the wealth and taste of the owner, and the skill of his
gardener. Structures were also developed to house specific types of novel
plants, such as camellias, as they were introduced into Britain. The terms
'orangery' and 'greenhouse' were not mutually exclusive and the two were
used for the same type of ornamental building in the 'polite' part of the
garden, housing tender 'greens' and flowering plants which would not
survive outdoors in the British climate.

The fashion for collecting citrus and other exotics gained great popularity
at the end of the seventeenth century with the arrival of King William III and
Queen Mary on the English throne. Sir Christopher Wren's rebuilding of
Hampton Court Palace for the joint monarchs included, in the main palace,
an orangery and grotto overlooking the new Privy Garden. A further

orangery was built by William Talman in the 1690s above the Pond Garden. Other glazed structures were constructed to house the queen's famous collection of 'exotics'. Talman also designed the 1st Duke's greenhouse at Chatsworth, Derbyshire in 1697. Although moved to a new site and slightly altered, this remains one of the most important surviving early greenhouses in the country.

Wren's royal Kensington Palace Orangery was a 'box' type of greenhouse of red and amber brick with thirteen openings across the south front. The three centre bays were set forward with a grand pediment above marking the entrance, leading into a fine interior. Others adapted this precedent, such as Vanbrugh's orangery at Stowe (c. 1720, now classrooms), comprising a high central block and lower flanking wings, all built in local stone.

In eighteenth-century Georgian gardens these refined boxes were largely rectangular in plan, built of masonry with a slate and tile roof, with large sash or removable windows on one side, which generally faced south to catch the maximum amount of precious sun. They might be free-standing or set into a garden wall or attached to the mansion. They were heated with a coal-fired boiler which in winter required the constant attention of a stoker.

Robert Adam's great Temple Greenhouse (1760) at Croome Court, Worcestershire, was built from Painswick limestone and was his first garden building. The five huge windows divided by plain Doric columns were removable for the summer, and lay below a great ornamental pediment sculpted with festoons of fruit and flowers spilling out of a basket. It stands proudly in the pleasure ground facing the mansion across the park and was

Robert Adam's great Temple Greenhouse at Croome Court, Worcestershire (1760). The sash windows, long gone, have recently been replaced.

The Orangery, Kew (1761), built for Princess Augusta by William Chambers at the opposite end of the gardens to his great Pagoda.

Camellia house, Chiswick House (Samuel Ware, 1813), in an enclosed flower garden, recently restored and retaining many rare, early camellia plants.

used to display tender exotics from the 6th Earl of Coventry's collection grown elsewhere in the garden. Furnishing was also important in these cases, and Adam also supplied designs for garden stools with lion's paw feet. The slightly later Orangery at Compton Verney, Warwickshire (1769–70, now gone), variously attributed to Adam or Brown, closely resembled the Croome Temple Greenhouse.

Around the same time (*c.* 1761) at Kew Sir William Chambers built an even larger building, an orangery, but in less expensive brick, stuccoed to make it look like stone in what is today Kew Gardens. The Dowager Princess Augusta developed the gardens of the Richmond Lodge estate at Kew and used Chambers as her architectural advisor, with Lord Bute providing advice on the botanical collection. It was a vast building for such a purpose, seven large bays long, with rusticated walls and arched openings, the first and last bays being pedimented. Tradition has it, however, that it was never successful in cultivating oranges.

Wentworth Woodhouse, South Yorkshire, boasts two important glasshouses. The building now known as Lady Rockingham's Tea Room was originally designed by Henry Flitcroft *c.* 1738 as a greenhouse, which formed part of the attractions of the first Marquess of Rockingham's Menagerie. This building faced north, overlooking a bowling green, and was perhaps not well suited to horticultural activities. Accordingly, in the early nineteenth century, the second Marquess built a new Camellia House onto the rear, south-

The 100-metre long orangery at Margam Park (1780s), overlooks the orangery pond. Unlike the Kew orangery, it was well designed for the hundred or so citrus trees, being long and narrow with a series of twenty-seven tall windows to admit the winter light. The plain back wall contained fireplaces, from which hot air passed through flues. In its centre was the high door through fully grown trees would be wheeled into the garden.

facing elevation of the old greenhouse. This refined structure had nine, tall sash windows separated by Ionic pilasters, and a glazed roof was intended specifically for the cultivation of camellias, which had only recently been introduced to cultivation in Britain and at the time were not considered to be hardy. Another early Camellia House (1813) can be found at Chiswick House, Middlesex. Overlooking an enclosed flower garden designed by Lewis Kennedy, this structure was built for the 6th Duke of Devonshire by Samuel Ware, and still retains many rare, early camellia plants.

Ornamental greenhouses and conservatories of various sizes and styles were an essential adjunct of the flower garden, allowing a wider range of plants to be grown, and also extending the period through which the garden could be enjoyed. Repton, often assisted by his architect sons George and John Adey, produced designs for conservatories and free-standing glasshouses in a variety of styles, to harmonise with the main house and the garden. The unrealised scheme for the Royal Pavilion,

The curved conservatory, Sezincote, the epitome of Indian style in gardens.

Brighton, included glazed corridors to serve as winter gardens; similar features were proposed for Woburn Abbey, Bedfordshire. The conservatory at Sezincote, Gloucestershire (*c.* 1800–5), on which Repton is believed to have collaborated with the architect S. P. Cockerell and the artist Thomas Daniell, is a similar corridor structure, curving gently from the house to an octagonal pavilion which originally served as an aviary. The building is lit by tall windows in Mogul style, echoing the extraordinary oriental architecture of the house, which is believed to have inspired the Prince Regent to build the Brighton Pavilion.

Throughout the early nineteenth century attention was focused on improving the design and efficiency of glazed structures for growing plants. Writers such as J. C. Loudon promoted a variety of designs and glazing systems through the pages of journals such as the *Gardener's Magazine*. The introduction of cast iron particularly revolutionised glasshouse construction, allowing – literally – new heights to be reached.

By the end of the period, in the 1820s and 1830s, completely glass-clad structures became technically possible, with so-called curvilinear glass encasing a cast-iron frame. These true glass houses not only had a stunning new billowing form but also greatly improved conditions for cultivating plants, with the increase in light levels all year round.

The monumental domed conservatory at Syon House, Middlesex (*c.* 1827–30), is perhaps the first significant metallic horticultural structure in the world. Designed by the architect Charles Fowler (best known for his contemporary Covent Garden Market) and Robert Forrest, Head Gardener

The conservatory at Syon House, Middlesex (*c.* 1827) is perhaps the first significant metallic horticultural structure in the world.

The Palm House, Bicton, Devon (early nineteenth century) formed the foundation for further innovation in glasshouse design.

to the Duke of Northumberland, the conservatory comprises a parabolic dome rising above the central section, and is flanked by curving wings leading to end pavilions. The utilitarian iron structure is partially disguised by ornamental stonework, but the engineering skill required to make this innovative building succeed is evident. Structures such as this, and the marginally more modest Palm House at Bicton, Devon (1820–5), formed the foundation for further innovation in the nineteenth century.

The Orangery at Wrest Park (1835) reflects the French Louis XV style of the mansion, which was rebuilt around the same time.

# THE ORIENT

ORIENTAL STYLES, derived from the countries of Asia, were popular in many respects with the Georgians in both home and garden. They came as a relief from the heavy Palladian and Baroque, and the other main alternative, Gothic (although sometimes the difference between Oriental

The Pagoda at Alton Towers, Staffordshire (Robert Abraham, 1826–30s) was modelled on the To-ho pagoda at Canton, and made from Coalbrookdale cast iron.

and Gothic became somewhat blurred). In the Georgian garden, oriental styles were used alongside rustic, Classical and other garden buildings, notably early on at Princess Augusta's garden at Kew, Surrey, to evoke many different associations.

During the eighteenth century Chinese and Indian styles and forms were gradually being reported in Europe, in a fairly sketchy and inaccurate manner in most cases, but they were embraced with enthusiasm and adapted to the European world. In the British landscape China found greatest favour, and Chinese seats, bridges and houses, tea houses and pagodas abounded in many forms, mostly light, airy and whimsical. They were then taken up in gardens all over Europe, with a surprisingly strong

William and John Halfpenny's design for a Chinese garden alcove, 1751.

following in Sweden, leading to a Continental style of gardening known as the 'Anglo-Chinoise'. To the Georgians the distinction between styles of various countries was not rigid, and Chinese, Moorish or Turkish might bear a considerable similarity to each other.

Things took off in Chinese style during the 1750s when several books of designs were published, including William and John Halfpenny's *New Designs for Chinese Bridges, Temples, Triumphal Arches, Garden Seats, Obelisks, Termini's &c* (1751). The most famous, and at the time, the most reliable of these was the royal architect Sir William Chambers' *Designs of Chinese Buildings, Furniture* … (1757). He wins the prize for the greatest Chinoiserie garden building of all, the muscular ten-storey pagoda at Kew (1761), which still dominates Kew Gardens amongst the later botanic planting. The pagoda was perhaps the most well-known symbol of Chinoiserie – even more so than the bridge and tea house. This atypically hefty octagonal tower of stock bricks, with ten roofs, and originally dragons and bells on the eaves, dominated the flat Surrey countryside in this area way beyond the circuit path around the Princess's *ferme ornée*, and must have presented an extraordinary sight. Other pagodas were built but none with the ambition of the Kew monster. Even an aspiring Warwickshire squire such as John Ludford of Ansley Hall could build a pagoda derived from Chambers' illustrations in 1767, which fell victim to the expansion of coal mining in the 1870s.

William Chambers'
Chinese Pagoda
for Princess
Augusta at Kew,
on the circuit walk
around her now
lost *ferme ornée*,
but since the
nineteenth century
it has terminated
the formal Pagoda
Vista from the
Palm House.

The late pagoda at Alton Towers (1820s), standing in a valley pool, is a far more attractive and charming building than that at Kew, even though it only reached three storeys of the intended six. It was to be as elaborate, if not more so, but never acquired the proposed forty gas-illuminated Chinese lanterns, dragons spouting water, and a jet some 22 metres high soaring from its top.

Early Chinese buildings at Kew included a House of Confucius and a Chinese arch (c. 1749) by Goupy, to which Chambers added the pagoda, a Chinese-style aviary (c. 1760) and a little airy octagonal open-sided pavilion in a pond.

House of Confucius (1740s), Kew, by Goupy for Princess Augusta, was an early oriental garden building.

Shugborough, Staffordshire, has a typical modest-sized but early Chinese tea house (1747), a small box built originally alongside a hexagonal six-storey timber pagoda (long gone). The tea house has fretwork-glazed windows and central double doors, and a roof curved down on all four sides over the single room, to turn upwards as a great overhang. Perhaps the eaves were embellished with bells. Typically, it was highly ornamented in Chinoiserie inside, even if plainer outside. The timber tea house at Stowe, Buckinghamshire (c. 1738), has a remarkable survival of highly-coloured, intricately-painted panels both inside and outside, depicting Chinese scenes, and lattice windows.

Later, much more ambitious 'Chinese' buildings were erected for George IV on the side of Virginia Water, Surrey: the magnificent Fishing Temple (c. 1825), based on an initial design by Sir Jeffry Wyatville, was full of gilt dragons, fretwork and little bells; there was a similar boat-house nearby (both demolished). A slightly more restrained essay in Chinoiserie had been built by the Duke of Cumberland at Virginia Water in the early 1750s. This tile-clad building with stained glass windows and lavish interior comprised three linked octagonal cells, each under elaborate 'Chinese' roofs with projecting eaves. The site of this building is known to this day as China Island. To go with his 'Chinese House', the Duke had a Thames hulk converted into the 'Mandarin Yacht' or 'Chinese Junk' in 1753, on which he could ply Virginia Water.

Chinese tents were more portable and ephemeral structures intended for outdoor entertaining; the one which survives at Boughton House, Northamptonshire, was originally re-erected in the garden of Montagu House, London, every summer. Some structures were little more than

The Chinese
pavilion and bridge
at Shugborough,
Staffordshire.

glorified 'umbrellos' under which a seat could be sheltered. The Chinese Seat at Hestercombe, Somerset, is more substantial, inviting the visitor to sit and contemplate the view across the combe. Its creator, Coplestone Warre Bampfylde, would certainly have known Cumberland's buildings at Virginia

Water; and to increase the 'oriental' character of the area around the Seat, he planted *Robinia* (false acacia), the craggy outline of which as it matured was considered to reflect the images of trees found on Chinese ceramics.

In the mid-eighteenth century so-called 'Chinese' bridges proliferated across lakes of all shapes and sizes. They were probably so popular because the requisite fretwork, or more commonly just criss-cross, of the timber parapet, conferring the Chinese character, was easy for the estate carpenter to knock up from a pattern book. Examples of the criss-cross pattern included Painshill, Surrey, and Ditchley, Oxfordshire – along with a sham bridge and a temple, both on a gently curved boarded footway – contrasting with the dizzying heights of the large and steeply curved bridge at Wotton Underwood, Buckinghamshire. As befitted a royal domain, the parapets of the timber bridges leading to the Duke of Cumberland's China Island at Virginia Water, Surrey, appear to have been executed in a more elaborate fretwork design; an example of this style of balustrade can still be seen on the Chinese Bridge at Penicuik House, Lothian.

The restored Turkey Building at Wotton Underwood, Buckinghamshire (now renamed the Turkish Kiosk), a wooden garden pavilion overlooking the 1750s 'Capability' Brown layout on his circuit walk around two large lakes.

The flamboyant Turkish Tent at Painshill is prominent on a wooded hillside overlooking the lake.

Opposite page and inset: The Indian bridge at Sezincote, Gloucestershire, is embellished with fine sculptures and sacred bulls.

The Near East was represented by what were supposed to be Moorish and Turkish styles. The Turkey Building (1750s, now renamed the Turkish Kiosk) appeared at Wotton Underwood overlooking the *ferme ornée* from Brown's circuit walk. At Painshill, Surrey, Charles Hamilton erected a Turkish Tent (1760), recently rebuilt, on a promontory overlooking the lake and Gothic Umbrello. It is an intriguing construction with a brick interior clothed in coarse painted cloth to achieve the look of a lavish tent. Not to be outdone, George IV created an entire 'Tented Encampment' in the Turkish style close to the Fishing Pavilion, Virginia Water. For the circuit walk at Kew Chambers designed a pavilion called the Alhambra (built in 1758 and long gone) with a Moorish fretwork balcony around the roof-top viewing platform, and a Mosque with minarets and a broad shallow dome; both were boldly painted and enlivened the scene considerably.

The Indian style was not prevalent in the Georgian garden, and only really puts in an appearance in the early nineteenth century. At Sezincote, Gloucestershire, where the Indian influence makes a great impact, Sir Charles Cockerell sought historical authenticity. The otherwise boxy house, topped by an onion dome, was designed by his brother S. P. Cockerell with advice from Thomas Daniell and his son William, the Indian topographical artists, and is thought to be the only surviving Mogul-style building in Western Europe. It has a curved orangery attached (*see* Orangeries and Conservatories), curving around the garden, with fifteen 'peacock-tail'-style window arches and other embellishments in Hindu and Mogul taste. The garden and park, on which Repton also advised, contains a collection of more features based on Indian precedent than any other. These include the Temple of Surya overlooking a pool with an Indian fountain, an Indian bridge carrying

The Temple and fountain of Surya, Sezincote, part of the Indian-themed garden.

the drive and containing seats below, with Brahmin bulls sitting on the balustrade, and a fountain with a bronze three-headed snake curving around a tree trunk below. In the park the extensive Home Farm was built in a simplified Indian style, *c.* 1800–5 by S. P. Cockerell and Thomas Daniell, and was enclosed by long buttressed walls giving the impression of a Mogul fort.

# ROTUNDAS

AN OPEN GARDEN ROTUNDA or rotondo looks like something from the top of a wedding cake: a graceful cylindrical confection of columns and a dome, it began as a rare and exquisite Georgian garden building, but is now familiar to most visitors to country houses. The rotunda was a circular Classical building, usually with a dome sheltering an open circle surrounded by columns, and was among the most versatile and popular of garden buildings as it could be cheaply built but still look substantial and impress visitors. As a non- (and also multi-) directional cylinder it was a useful pivot point within the garden layout. Rotundas could either be open (monopteral)

The circular Temple of Vesta (1st century BC) at Tivoli, a Roman hilltop resort outside Rome. It is one of the main models for the rotunda, which epitomises the English landscape garden.

or closed (peripteral), the latter having a central cylindrical wall. Both forms were based on antique precedent; the open form was based on the circular Greek temple of Venus at Cnidus with Praxiteles' statue of the Venus Pudica. Similar Roman examples were more familiar to eighteenth-century Grand Tourists, including the temples of Vesta in Rome and Tivoli.

Open rotundas mushroomed in poularity during the eighteenth century, the dome, supported on spindly columns, often sheltering a statue. Some had exquisitely decorated domed ceilings.

They usually had between eight and twelve columns in one of the Classical orders (Ionic, Tuscan and Corinthian being popular). Vanbrugh's lost example at Castle Howard, Yorkshire, was one of the earliest as a garden building (*c.* 1715), similar to the Rotondo he then designed at Stowe, Buckinghamshire,

The Rotondo at Stowe (Sir John Vanbrugh, 1720–1) is one of the earliest garden rotundas, and an early example of the neo-classical style in gardens. It is based on the Hellenistic temple of Venus at Cnidus and contained a gilt statue of the goddess.

*c.* 1720, which was probably the most influential on later similar garden structures (it was remodelled in the 1760s). An oddity was Charles

The Panorama, Croome Court, is a late example of a closed rotunda, designed by James Wyatt in 1801 and built in 1805–12. It is one of four large outlying eyecatchers beyond the edge of the huge park.

Hamilton's octagonal Gothic Temple at Painshill, Surrey: essentially an open Classical rotunda in form, it was built (cheaply, of timber painted to look like stone) in Gothic style with ogee arches, at the top of a steep turf slope overlooking the pleasure ground and lake spread out below.

The Petworth Rotunda, Sussex, is a typical open example. When newly built it was seen by Earl Temple of Stowe in 1766: 'The day we arrived [at Petworth] was distinguished by the finishing a little Rotondo, something larger however, than that at Hagley'. He was enthusiastic about its positioning as it 'fairly beats upon the whole in point of situation all the Rotondos I have seen'. This was praise indeed from a man with his own very early garden rotunda and who owned and continued to develop one of the greatest Georgian gardens. The Petworth Rotunda was similar to the remodelled Stowe Rotondo, with ten columns and a shallow dome, but it seems not to have had a statue.

Closed or filled (peripteral) rotundas were perhaps less common because they were more expensive to build. They were built in a variety of garden situations. Kent's Temple of Ancient Virtue at Stowe (1730s) overlooks his sweeping and deeply picturesque Elysian Fields and the Temple of British Worthies. By contrast, the Round House at Bramham, Yorkshire (*c*. 1740s) stands at a *rond point* at the heart of a formal French-style layout, and is scaled to act as a focus in distant views. A series of routes leads through woodland from the Round House, linking with another *rond point* dominated by a large obelisk. At Castle Howard the

The Round House,
Bramham,
Yorkshire
(c. 1740s), a closed
rotunda, at a *rond
point* at the heart
of a formal French-
style layout, scaled
to act as a focus in
distant views.

The Ionic Temple
at Wentworth
Woodhouse,
is unusual in its
choice of
masculine resident:
Hercules fighting a
dragon, rather than
the more usual
statue of Venus.

Mausoleum (Hawksmoor and others, 1729–40), is a massive domed monument over 30 metres high encircled by twenty columns. It is one of Hawksmoor's best-known and most striking provincial works, built as a stark landmark in the park. These dramatic buildings remained popular for the wealthiest owners throughout the Georgian period ranging from the very early Doric (or Tuscan) Temple built at the end of a garden terrace at Duncombe Park, North Yorkshire (attributed to Sir Thomas Robinson, *c.* 1730) and The Panorama on a hill in the park at Croome Court (designed by James Wyatt, 1801, built 1805–12).

The Mussenden Temple, Downhill, County Derry (1783–5), is surely the most breathtakingly sited rotunda (its drama equal to that of the Temple of Vesta at Tivoli itself), for it stands precariously perched on cliffs 60 metres above the Atlantic Ocean on the north coast of Ulster. The Bishop of Derry and Earl of Bristol (the Earl Bishop) built this closed rotunda to be seen from the house, as he hoped: 'Elegant, exquisite, looking towards the sea. Below there will be a drop of hundreds of feet onto the strand of Magilligan … It is to have a library and a crypt underneath.'

Rotundas were often dedicated to a concept, such as Fame, or a Classical figure, such as Venus (Stowe) or Hercules (Wentworth Woodhouse). Rotundas dedicated to Fame were modelled on the design and position of the antique Temple of Vesta on the edge of the cliff at Tivoli outside Rome, and indicated a moral lesson for visitors. Apollo pointed the way up the difficult, rocky path to reach the female figure of Fame in her open rotunda, as illustrated in Maratta's painting at Stourhead. The rotunda on top of a cliff at Studley Royal (1729, rebuilt *c.* 1780) was dedicated to Fame. Others at the top of a steep slope included Petworth, Hall Barn (Buckinghamshire), and The Temple of Apollo at Stourhead.

The Mussenden Temple, Downhill, Co. Derry (1783–85), surely the most breathtakingly positioned rotunda (its drama equal to that of the Temple of Vesta at Tivoli itself), precariously perched on cliffs 60m above the Atlantic Ocean on the north coast of Ulster.

# RUINS

R UINS were built to last, despite their air of decrepitude. When an owner was unable to boast a genuine ruined medieval building to remind others of his long pedigree and his family's attachment to its land, he built one, and generally it was pretty solidly constructed. Ruins were valued for their ability to evoke the medieval, as Horace Walpole put it, 'the true rust of the Barons' Wars', and many were erected, not just in the increasingly popular Gothic style, but deliberately distressed to evoke the air of centuries of neglect and periodic abuse. In this form they mixed antiquity, the Gothic and the playful to provide an eccentric ornament. Ruins in the garden were more light-hearted in their function, often used as a summerhouse, than ruins constructed in the park which usually had a more serious use such as a farm building or staff housing, hiding behind the ruined façade.

The entrance to the chalk caves (in effect a giant grotto) at West Wycombe (1750s), doubled as a ruined church eye-catcher on the hill above the house, garden and park below.

Alfred's Hall, Cirencester Park, Gloucestershire is one of the first sham ruins, completed by 1721. Its authenticity was noted approvingly by Mrs Delaney in 1733 after the addition of various medieval features from a nearby manor house: 'It is now a venerable castle and has been taken by an antiquarian as one of King Arthur's.'

An early and appealing sham Gothic ruin is at Fawley Court, Buckinghamshire. In 1731 John Freeman built his Thamesside Gothic Ruin, a small ruined flint 'church', around a domed room with a sheeps' knucklebone floor to house his collection of Arundel Marbles: antique Greek and Roman sculptures. To give it some authenticity at least, he inserted a perpendicular window from a nearby church into a wall, and embowered it in a gloomy pleasure ground planted with yew and box. Nearby, at West Wycombe in the 1750s, Sir Francis Dashwood built a paradox to this (possibly a parody): a cruder ecclesiastical flint façade as the great extrovert entrance to his notorious chalk Hellfire Caves.

Sanderson Miller was the master of the park ruin for several decades from the 1740s, having an antiquarian's eye for authenticity. He designed the ruined castle at Hagley Hall, Worcestershire (1747–8). William Shenstone wrote that 'it consists of one entire Tow'r and three stumps of Tow'rs with a ruined wall betwixt them. There is no great art or variety in ye Ruin, but the situation gives it a charming effect.' It became an instant and celebrated success, influential for the rest of the century, particularly when the Picturesque movement took up the idea of ruins. Again genuine medieval fabric was used, this time windows from Halesowen Abbey, and the patina of age encouraged. Miller, a gentleman amateur, designed other ruins including the similar Gothic Tower, Wimpole Hall, Cambridgeshire, built much later as a distant eyecatcher from the house in Lancelot Brown's park. Both these and their direct progeny such as the Drayton Arch, Wroxton, Oxfordshire (c. 1770s) and The Spectacle, Boughton, Northamptonshire (c. 1770) occupied smoothly landscaped Brownian parks.

The Ruined Castle, Hagley Hall, Worcestershire (1747–8), oozing with, as Horace Walpole put it, 'the true Rust of the Barons' wars'. It was very influential on other owners, many of whom erected their own garden and park 'ruins'.

The Spectacle, Boughton, Northants (c. 1770) is a theatrical structure, framing the drive and the entrance to the park. It is very similar to the contemporary Drayton Arch at Wroxton, Oxfordshire.

Ruggedness and asymmetry were key to the Picturesque movement, and ruins formed a natural part of this. In Yorkshire, ruins – both genuine and sham – abounded in parks and gardens. Here, as everywhere else, when genuine medieval ruins were available they were drawn into the design with enthusiasm. The Aislabies at Studley Royal, Yorkshire, used the medieval Fountains Abbey ruins as the most enormous, and genuinely ancient, garden feature, seen at the end of a valley. Nearby at Duncombe Park the Rievaulx Terrace along the cliff top between two refined banqueting pavilions had numerous views of another ruined medieval abbey below. Elsewhere in Yorkshire the Aislabies constructed Mowbray Castle, an early faux 'ruin', in a pleasure ground at Hackfall. It was perhaps inspired by The King's Tower, Knaresborough Castle, which had been in a semi-demolished state for over a hundred years. The octagonal Gothic building (c. 1750s) has a jagged, ruined masonry outline with cross loops along its upper floor, on a cliff high above the valley of the River Ure.

At Croome Court, Worcestershire, two large 'medieval' ruins were built at distant, opposite ends of the estate. The military-cum-ecclesiastical Dunstall Castle (1784) has three tall, cylindrical towers (one ruined) between two walls including a ruined gateway, just visible from the house

Mowbray Castle, Hackfall, North Yorkshire (c. 1750), an early faux 'ruin', in a rugged pleasure ground, was perhaps inspired by The King's Tower at Knaresborough Castle, which had been in a semi-demolished state for over one hundred years.

across the park. Pirton Tower (James Wyatt, 1801) is a ruined stone curtain wall of deeply craggy outline, perched high on a shoulder of land in a detached park, with a central tower housing a small spiral staircase to a viewing platform.

Ruins were occasionally built in a Classical, rather than a Gothic style. A vast composition was created of arches, columns

Pirton Tower (James Wyatt, 1801), adds a dramatic Gothic flavour when seen from Croome Court park. It comprises only a curtain wall with a central spiral staircase to a small viewing platform.

Dunstall Castle, Croome Court, Worcestershire (1784), with Pirton Tower, is one of four great outlying eyecatchers of this estate.

Columns from the Roman ruins of Leptis Magna, Libya, were moved to Virginia Water in the 1820s.

and lintels from the great city of Leptis Magna (in what is now Libya) for George IV in Windsor Great Park next to Virginia Water in the late 1820s, flanking the drive up to Fort Belvedere. It occupies an area some 70 metres by 30 metres, with columns 10 metres high and is one of the most impressive artificial ruins in Britain, but is, even so, only a fragment of the original city.

# TEMPLES AND PAVILIONS

A LL SELF-RESPECTING Georgian gardens had at least one temple or pavilion on the circuit path. It was generally designed as a summerhouse and certainly intended as an ornament to the scene. The terms 'temple', 'pavilion' and 'summerhouse' were largely interchangeable, depending on the whim of the owner, and sometimes how the building fitted in with the allusions within the whole garden. A temple had no serious religious use, but reflected its dedication by the owner to an ancient deity, a particular event or concept. Most were single- or two-storey buildings and some were very finely decorated. Their placing in the landscape was important not just to allow prospects of the scenery from within, but also often to be seen to best advantage as part of the scenery from a distance. In this way a west-facing building would shine out in the evening sun, while an east-facing one was seen at its best in the morning and then might perhaps disappear from the scenery.

These buildings were used on the circuit walk or at extremities of the design as shelter from the unpredictable British weather, for picnics and banquets, or just as a remote retreat from the throng in the mansion, as well as providing a feature in the landscape. They were often sited at the edge of the landscape design by a ha-ha to take in wider views and 'borrowed landscape' owned by others but appropriated in views. Some, such as Kent's Temple of Venus at Stowe (*c.* 1732), were specifically intended for amorous trysts or other less family-oriented activities requiring seclusion.

Temples were dedicated to deities, concepts, mortals or even battles. Bacchus (god of wine) was invoked at Stowe and Painshill, and Venus (goddess of love) was found at Stowe.

Vanbrugh's Temple of Bacchus, Stowe (1720s), was a focal point of the Garden of Vice, embowered in hanging yews and standing opposite the Temple of Venus across the lake.

One of a pair of Tuscan temples flanking a lake at Wotton Underwood, Bucks: small, timber pavilions with a portico on each side sheltering a seat, looking in opposite directions.

The Temple of Theseus, Hagley, stands remote above the mansion, facing south at the top of a slope, framed by trees, with views across Hagley Park and to the hills beyond.

At Stourhead the focal Pantheon (Henry Flitcroft, 1753–4) was originally dedicated to the mortal Hercules, whose statue it housed, its form recalling its prototype in Rome, one of the best preserved and admired of Roman buildings. It is overlooked across the lake by another large stone temple, that

of Apollo (Flitcroft, 1765), a version of the round temple illustrated in
Wood's *Ruins of Balbec* (1757). The Temple of Theseus (1758) at Hagley,
Worcestershire, was designed by James 'Athenian' Stuart (1713–88)
following his return from Athens and was dedicated to the mortal who slew
the legendary Minotaur. Conceived as a miniature replica of a Greek Doric
temple, the building faces south at the top of a slope, framed by trees, with
views across Hagley Park and to the hills beyond. It is one of the earliest
Greek Doric Revival buildings.

Some temples had less specific Classical dedications, such as the Satyr's
Temple, Castle Hill, Devon (*c.* 1740), which along with the Sybil's Cave and the
unfortunately named Ugly Bridge (a rustic stone bridge) form a group of
structures in Earl Clinton's important pleasure grounds created between
*c.* 1720 and 1751. Vanbrugh designed the Temple of the Winds (1724) at Castle
Howard, based on Palladio's famous sixteenth-century Villa Rotonda at Vicenza
in Italy. It stands overlooking the park, exposed to the four winds at the end of

Nicholas Revett's curved-fronted Temple of Music, West Wycombe Park, Bucks (1770s) occupies an Arcadian island in the lake surrounded by the Chiltern hills, which are hard to beat for a beautiful setting.

Kent's Temple of British Worthies (c. 1735) stands in the Elysian Fields opposite his Temple of Ancient Virtue (and formerly that of Modern Virtue, symbolically a ruin), both reflected across the smooth lawns in the Worthies river which divided them.

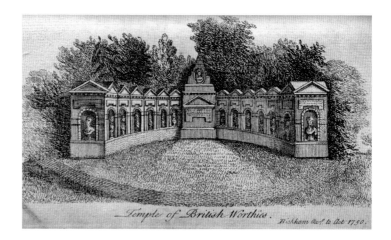

a long garden terrace from the mansion, with porticos sheltering its four sides. West Wycombe has a curved-fronted Music Temple on an Arcadian island in the lake surrounded by the Chiltern hills which is hard to beat for its setting.

Stowe cannot be ignored as it was so influential and, of its three dozen or more garden buildings, had temples dedicated to many concepts as well as Classical deities. These included, in the Elysian Fields, those to Ancient and Modern Virtue (both Kent, 1730s), the latter a symbolic ruin and now gone; one of its greatest temples is dedicated to Concord [sic] and Victory (1749) commemorating British victories in the largely forgotten Seven Years' War against France (1756–63). Overlooking the Grecian Valley, Concord and Victory is the first building in England designed to imitate Greek architecture. Perhaps the most unusual of Stowe's temples is the curving golden stone wall called the Temple of British Worthies (William Kent, c. 1735), in the Elysian Fields overlooking the Alder River and the Temple of Ancient Virtue. Based on a Roman precedent taken up by Palladio, it contains fourteen busts in a row of niches including monarchs, poets, men of action and philosophers, with a bust of Mercury above to lead the Worthies to the Elysian Fields. It is surely no coincidence that the family name of Stowe's creators was indeed Temple.

Fawley Court Island Temple is a two-storey Adam temple in a watery situation on an island commanding a view up the Thames at Henley. It is an eyecatcher from the mansion, gardens, park and surrounding Chilterns.

Some of the prettiest temples and summerhouses are oval. The Terrace or Oval Temple, Farnborough, Warwickshire, is a Classical, two-storey pavilion half-way up the great gently sloping terrace overlooking the Warmington valley and Edgehill beyond, which now shines out when viewed from the M40 motorway in the evening sun. It was designed by local gentleman architect Sanderson Miller and built by William Hiorn for William Holbech (c. 1750) of ironstone with limestone dressings and a domed roof. The ground floor has an open loggia of four Tuscan columns and an oval stone table. The first-floor 'Prospect Room' is reached from the rear via an external curving stone staircase and has curved sash windows, fine rococo plasterwork between the windows and in the dome, and an ornamental wooden floor. It forms an important feature of the Terrace Walk, which is probably also by Sanderson Miller, a major example of mid-eighteenth-century landscape design. The Farnborough terrace originally extended to what must have been one of the most unusually designed temples: the Pentagon Temple – a two-storey affair with an arcaded lower storey supporting an upper room with a balustrade. This temple stood in its own enclosed flower garden.

Most temples were Classical in style, and some were simply named after their type of architectural style, particularly Doric, Ionic and Tuscan temples. Examples include the Doric Temple at Bowood, Wiltshire (c. 1800), the Ionic and Tuscan temples (c. 1758) at either end of the curving Rievaulx Terrace, North Yorkshire, and the Ionic Temple which forms another feature on the terrace at Farnborough, Warwickshire.

Rarely, buildings called temples were derived from medieval northern European Gothic, a contradiction in terms as Gothic was a Christian style. At Stowe, James Gibbs built the large, triangular Gothic Temple (1741) of orangey ironstone, with its three turrets (one with a belvedere) and central domed ceiling, commanding the Eastern Gardens.

The Ionic Seat, Wilton, is very similar to those at Hartwell (gone), Hall Barn and in Gibbs's pattern book (1728).

Gibbs's Gothic Temple, Stowe (1741), is built of rusty ironstone on top of the Hawkwell Hill and has panoramic views of many other garden and park monuments and buildings in the distance.

Sometimes a martial dedication was called for; after all, Britain was at war for much of the Georgian period and many owners were military men. The stone Blenheim Pavilion (1720s) at Cliveden, Buckinghamshire, stands high above the Thames, originally terminating a long green walk from the mansion (it now overlooks an informal lawn). Leoni's single-roomed building has an open front in the form of a triumphal arch decorated with military trophies in relief, designed for Lord Orkney, one of the Duke of Marlborough's generals, to commemorate the great victory in the Battle of Blenheim in 1704.

Phelps's design for a bowling-green house for Mr Bampfylde (c.1750), probably at Hestercombe, Somerset.

Sporting pavilions were common, particularly for the bowling greens which proliferated, such as at Gobions, Hertfordshire (c. 1730s). Bridgeman's bowling green was surrounded by clipped yew hedges, with a small, square, domed summerhouse on a bank at one end (now gone). The

rendered brick, castellated Gothic Pavilion (c. 1740) overlooks the large bowling green at Hall Barn, Buckinghamshire, framed by a tall, clipped yew hedge.

By the early nineteenth century, while Classical architecture remained popular for temples, much of the Classical symbolism with which they had been endowed in the previous century had been abandoned. A pair of Corinthian temples at Castle Hill, Devon (1831), on the eastern and western sides of the pleasure grounds, are known respectively as the Sunrise and Sunset Temple, emphasising the role of the temple as a place of rest and refreshment within the landscape.

# TOWERS: PROSPECT AND ASPECT

Towers offered prospect and commanded aspect. Georgian prospect towers originated from hunting lodges and viewing towers in Tudor and Stuart deer parks with excellent panoramic views, such as Robert Smythson's Hunting Tower high above the park at Chatsworth, Derbyshire (1580s). In the Georgian park and garden they became eyecatchers within the design, often on top of a hill, dominating their surrounds. Visible from the countryside way beyond, a looming presence heralded the taste and wealth of the owner many miles from his power base within the park.

As prospect towers they offered excellent bird's-eye and panoramic views of the park and the owner's estate beyond, building on the illusion (reinforced by the ubiquitous ha-ha) that he owned the countryside for as far as the eye could see. The more counties that could be seen, the better; at Broadway Tower, the outlying eyecatcher for Croome Park some 15 miles away, it was claimed that twelve counties could be seen. Size mattered. The higher the tower and the more storeys, the better to impress visiting friends and relatives. One of the tallest and most detailed in its ornamentation is Brizlee Tower on a hill in Hulne Park, Alnwick, overlooking much of north Northumberland. It was designed by Robert Adam in 1777 and erected in the 'Capability' Brown park *c.* 1781 for Hugh Percy, 1st Duke of Northumberland. Sometimes a tower would house an estate worker's family, such as the circular Gothic Bourbon Tower, Stowe (Gibbs, 1740), which was a lodge for the deer keeper, but often it was purely for the pleasure of the family, their visitors and tourists.

Painshill Park, Surrey: the mid-eighteenth-century Gothic Tower, intended to evoke Parliamentary liberty and, like many other such towers, placed in a distant part of the park on a high point with stunning views from the upper storeys.

Broadway Tower, Worcestershire, the farthest outlier for Croome Court some fifteen miles away, a 'Saxon' tower by James Wyatt (designed 1790s). It stands on the second highest point of the Cotswolds.

Some towers occupied the heart of the landscape, perhaps even in the garden, such as the three-storey stone tower at Goldney, Bristol (1760s). Most, however, stood at the park boundary straddling the divide between the Arcadian landscape and the rude agricultural world beyond. Some, such as Broadway Tower, Worcestershire, and the cliff-top tower at Mount Edgcumbe, Cornwall (*see opposite*) were built way beyond the park on estate land as outliers. It was said that Broadway Tower, standing on one of the high points of the Cotswold scarp, was lit up when the 6th Earl of Coventry left his nearby country retreat for the palatial Croome Court in the vale, to warn the staff that he was on his way and make preparations to receive him. Best of all was when a great tower could be built on a high point so that no-one could miss it for miles around. It is difficult to see the severely plain and huge Alfred's Tower (1770s) at Stourhead, Somerset, from the wooded park in which it stands and not at all from the pleasure ground, but it is so tall it can be seen from the distant hills for miles around. It was the focal point of a long ride around the park laid out in the 1760s.

Cotehele, Cornwall, was abandoned by the Edgcumbe family in the seventeenth century in favour of the newly built Mount Edgcumbe overlooking Plymouth Sound. Towards the end of the eighteenth century, however, the family realised that Cotehele, which had been untouched for generations, possessed considerable antiquarian interest and charm. In preparation for a second visit from King George III and Queen Charlotte in 1789 (or perhaps to commemorate the creation of the Earldom of Mount Edgcumbe that year), a Gothic, triangular-plan prospect tower was built in the park. A second, more or less identical tower was built at the same time on the coastal carriage drive at Mount Edgcumbe, and signals could be passed

The Gothic Tower, Goldney House, Bristol, on a formal terrace above the grotto, dominates the garden.

from one tower to another, to announce, for example, that the family was leaving one residence to travel up or down the River Tamar to the other.

Towers took various forms. Some were square and clearly intended to mimic medieval fortifications such as the four-storey Painshill Park tower, Surrey (c. 1750). Others were circular, like the one above the engine house at Goldney, Bristol. If the owner was very lucky he might have a ready-made tower in his park with a genuine medieval origin, but often these were ruined, such as the centrepiece of Fountains Abbey, in the pleasure ground at Studley Royal, North Yorkshire. Owners were not beyond borrowing medieval towers beyond the park to terminate views with a genuinely antiquarian patina of

The Tower of the Winds, Athens, was embellished with a combination of sundials, a water clock and a wind vane. It was the model for several garden buildings, including at Shugborough, Mount Stewart, Northern Ireland, and West Wycombe, Buckinghamshire.

age, particularly church towers, the best being needle-like spires pointing heavenwards such as that at Fletching in East Sussex, seen in the view across Sheffield Park.

Mediterranean Classical elegance was favoured as well as native Gothic. The ancient Greek octagonal Tower of the Winds in Athens was used as a model several times from the 1750s when the buildings of Classical Greece became more widely known. An early example, the Temple of the Four Winds, for Sir Francis Dashwood by Nicholas Revett, linked the park and pleasure ground at West Wycombe, Buckinghamshire (1759). James 'Athenian' Stuart built a free-standing neoclassical Tower of the Winds at Shugborough, Staffordshire (1764) and another at Mount Stewart, County Down in Northern Ireland (c. 1780).

The most ungainly towers were triangular, including the massive Alfred's Tower, Stourhead, Wiltshire (1760s) and Hoober Stand, Wentworth

Woodhouse, South Yorkshire (Henry Flitcroft, 1746–8). In contrast, Brizlee Tower is a bristling skyrocket confection that inspired the duke's pastry chef.

Sometimes, as with temples and rotundas, the tower was dedicated to a person, idea or cause. The theme of Liberty preoccupied many Georgian garden-makers who espoused the Whig political cause. Alfred's Tower, Stourhead, celebrated King Alfred as a symbol of British liberty in a group of buildings dedicated to this theme in the park and pleasure ground. The Gothic Tower at Painshill also evoked Liberty. The Culloden Tower (1746), Richmond, Yorkshire, was named by the Hanoverian supporter John Yorke, to celebrate the English victory in the Scottish battle in 1745, and the Marquess of Rockingham's Hoober Stand similarly celebrated the Hanoverian monarchy and its builder's loyalty to the Crown, and commemorated the suppression of the Jacobite Rebellion in 1745 by King George II. Paxton's Tower, Carmarthenshire, was built in 1811 in Lord Nelson's honour.

Shugborough, Staffordshire: in contrast to the Saxon and Gothic connections this tower is firmly based on Classical precedent, the Tower of the Winds in Athens, newly published in the mid-eighteenth century by James 'Athenian' Stuart. Several others based on this model were built in gardens.

Below: Culloden Tower, Richmond, North Yorkshire, is a solid Gothic tower on high ground in a park but below the town of Richmond, making it prominent from the real medieval castle.

Right: The exquisitely decorated interior of the Culloden Tower belies its sombre martial exterior.

# WATERY DIVERSIONS: BOAT-HOUSES, BATH-HOUSES AND FISHING TEMPLES

WATER was essential in the best Georgian landscapes. Not just great sheets shimmering as lakes across parks and pleasure grounds, but more modestly, rivers, streams and smaller ponds too, together with the springs that bubbled up out of the ground to supply them. To make the most of the watery experience there were, of course, dedicated buildings reflecting the various ways to enjoy the water.

Boat-houses and fishing houses were for those who preferred aquatic activities without getting wet. For closer interaction with the water, the bath-house was for the more hardy who relished the health-giving properties of a cold dip in the privacy of their own grounds. Sometimes health-giving springs were enclosed ornamentally as a feature by a building or spring-head

The iron-rich Chaileybeate spring at Gayhurst, Buckinghamshire, emerges in a wood below a stone pedestal and urn (dated 1751), a surprise on a remote part of the walk to the river.

Robert Adam's Fishing Pavilion at Kedleston Hall, Derbyshire, forms part of a sweeping view across the park including the lake, Classical bridge and mansion.

for drinking the mineral-laden waters. At Gayhurst, Buckinghamshire, a small urn on a hefty stone pedestal (dated 1751) stands above the babbling Chaileybeate spring (its iron-rich water used to bathe the eyes) in a remote part of the pleasure ground on the way to the river.

Many bath-houses stood alongside a river or lake, including Lord Burlington's Palladian-style 'bagnio' alongside a quiet pond at Chiswick House, Middlesex (designed 1717), and the more rugged one of the 1780s at Downton in deepest Herefordshire, above the tumbling River Teme.

The most elaborate structures combined several functions, such as the early Water House, Carshalton House, Surrey (c. 1719–20). This garden eyecatcher combined a pretty tiled bathroom fed from a cistern in a sham church-tower, powered by a water-wheel, along with an orangery and a banqueting room. Adam's grand two-storey lakeside Fishing Pavilion (c. 1769) at Kedleston Hall, Derbyshire, built in his distinctive 'antique' style, had yet more water-related uses. A fishing and gaming room above is stylishly decorated with his typical plasterwork, and high-quality paintings of fishy and marine scenes. Below, at the level of the lake, two boat-houses open to the water flanking a spartan cold bath, reached by a double stair. The lakeside façade is the most imposing, to be seen from the lake and the surrounding grounds, and taken in from the park as part of a sweeping view of the mansion and bridge. Ornamental fishing pavilions seem to have been unusual, although a particularly exuberant example in the Chinese taste was created for George IV at Virginia Water, Surrey in the 1820s, along with a boat-house in similar style.

Like Kedleston, the grander bath-houses were of two storeys, with a gaming room cum summerhouse above a cold bath; but more modest structures were also built. The octagonal Bathing House on the banks of the River Dart at Sharpham, Devon (1769), comprised only a single dressing or refreshment room. Some bath-houses were of even more rudimentary design: William Kent's at Rousham, Oxfordshire, overlooking an octagonal pool fed by a serpentine rill, is essentially a rocky cavern to shelter the bathers when they emerged from the cold dark water.

A river or lakeside site for the bath-house was not essential: a spring would do, to feed the plunge pool within. At Walton Hall, Warwickshire, Sir Charles Mordaunt's two-storey bath-house (c. 1750) stands in woodland above the drive to the Hall, and enjoys surprise views over the park. This exquisite Georgian garden building contrasts a rusticated lower storey containing a watery grotto-like pool room, with a lavishly decorated

William Kent's pool house, Rousham, is a small grot for bathers to shelter in on emerging from the octagonal plunge pool in this secluded, shady part of the 1730s pleasure ground.

The Bath-house,
Walton Hall,
Warwickshire, has
a bright and richly
decorated
Classical drawing
room with long
views over the
park, above a dark
rugged grotto with
the plunge pool.

The lower storey
of the Walton
Bath-house is
richly decorated as
a gloomy grotto.

The Bath-house at Wrest Park, Bedfordshire, complete with 'ruin' and thatched cottage.

octagonal Palladian drawing room above, complete with dome, plaster stalactite frieze and shell festoons over the fireplace and windows.

Departing from the more usual Classical style, Brown designed a Gothic bathing house at Corsham Court, Wiltshire (1760s). Like Walton Hall, it is approached via a gloomy route to give a surprise view of the pleasure grounds from the dressing room above and in turn forms a feature in the garden. Bath-houses could even be conceived as picturesque ruins: the bath designed for Jemima, Marchioness Grey at Wrest Park, Bedfordshire, has an outdoor bath decorously screened by a 'ruin', while an attached thatched cottage provided a place for the bathers to recover from their immersion. The late eighteenth-century bath-house at Greenway, Devon, was also originally thatched to create a picturesque incident in the grounds. The stone-lined plunge bath chamber has a sitting room above with a balcony looking across the Dart.

Georgian boat-houses enclosed a dock on the shore of a lake or river. They seem to have been more the servants' domain than the gentleman's, but even so they usually contributed to the scene. One of the most sophisticated is at Fonthill, Wiltshire (mid-eighteenth century), by the lake, with a central dock and stone path around, leading to a domed circular

The Boat-house, Fonthill Splendens (c. 1750s) has a stone roof on which the reflected water sparkles, with a stone boss of icicles in the dome.

The Classical boat-house at Fyne Court, Somerset, disguises the end of the serpentine artificial river; it has a Gothic façade on the rear, woodland approach side.

rear, with a great central boss of icicles or stalactites. In the Lake District boat-houses embellished parks around the natural lakes, including the Earl of Surrey's at Lyulph's Tower, Ullswater, where the boats were kept to fire guns to generate sublime echoes across the lake.

While many boat-houses were Classical, others were Gothic or rustic, and some adopted more than one style. Sanderson Miller designed a Gothic boat-house at Enville Hall, Staffordshire, *c*. 1755. Towards the end of the century, two quite similar rustic or picturesque boat-houses were constructed at Port Eliot (1792) and Pentillie Castle (*c*. 1810), Cornwall. Humphry Repton advised at both estates, and probably designed the buildings. The contemporary boat-house at Stourhead appears, when seen across the lake, to be the rocky entrance to a cave.

The boat-house overlooking the River Tamar below Pentillie Castle, Cornwall, adopts a picturesque style, perhaps by Humphry Repton, who advised in 1810, and resembles another Cornish boat-house at Port Eliot.

# FURTHER READING

Adam, R. *The Works in Architecture of Robert and James Adam*. Dover, 1980.

Brown, J. *The Art and Architecture of English Gardens*. Rizzoli, 1989.

Buxbaum, T. *Icehouses*. Shire, 2008.

Dixon-Hunt, J. *William Kent Landscape Garden Designer*. Zwemmer, 1987.

*Garden History* (The Journal of the Garden History Society). 1965 onwards.

Gibbs, J. *Gibbs' Book of Architecture*. Dover, 2008.

Hadfield, M. *The English Landscape Garden*. Shire, 1997.

Howley, J. *The Follies and Garden Buildings of Ireland*. Yale, 1993.

Jackson, H. *Shell Houses and Grottoes*. Shire, 2001.

Jackson-Stops, G. *An English Arcadia 1600–1990*. The National Trust, 1992.

Jones, B. *Follies & Grottoes*. Constable, 2nd edn. 1974.

Lambton, L. *Palaces for Pigs: Animal Architecture and other Beastly Buildings*. English Heritage, 2011.

*Landmark Trust Handbook*. Landmark Trust. 24th edn. 2011 onwards.

Mayer, L. *Capability Brown and the English Landscape Garden*. Shire, 2011.

Papworth, J. B. *Rural Residences ... for Cottages, Small Villas and Other Ornamental Buildings*. Elibron Classics, 2005.

Pevsner, N. *Pevsner's Architectural Glossary*. Yale, 2010.

Ridgway, C. and R. Williams. *Sir John Vanbrugh and Landscape Architecture*. Sutton, 2000.

Rolf, V. *Bathing Houses and Plunge Pools*. Shire, 2011.

Rowan, A. *Garden Buildings*. R.I.B.A. Drawings series, 1968.

Sir John Soane's Museum. *A Passion for Building, The Amateur Architect in England 1650–1850*. Sir John Soane's Museum, 2007.

Symes, M. *A Glossary of Garden History*. Shire, 2nd edn. 2006.

Tames, Richard. *Robert Adam*. Shire, 2004.

*The Follies Journal*. The Journal of the Folly Fellowship, 1988 onwards.

Whitelaw, J. *Follies*. Shire, 2005.

Yorke, Trevor. *British Architectural Styles: An Easy Reference Guide*. Countryside Books, 2008.

## WEBSITES

*See* Places to Visit, below, for web addresses of individual sites.

Images of England (listed buildings): www.imagesofengland.org.uk

The Garden History Society: www.gardenhistorysociety.org.uk

The Association of Gardens Trusts: www.gardenstrusts.org.uk

The Georgian Group: www.georgiangroup.org.uk

The Folly Fellowship: www.follies.org.uk

The Landmark Trust: www.landmarktrust.org.uk

The Landmark Trust has many fine Georgian garden buildings that it lets out for holidays, some of which have been mentioned above, including the Netherby Salmon Coop, Walton Bath-house, The Gothic Temple (Stowe), Clytha Castle (Monmouthshire), and Culloden Tower (North Yorkshire). More details can be found in their handbook and on their website.

# PLACES TO VISIT

The following gardens and parks open to the public are selected for the number and range of Georgian garden buildings they contain. Most were famed in the eighteenth century for their gardens and garden buildings.

ENGLAND

Antony House, Torpoint, PL11 2QA. Telephone: 01752 812191.
  Website: www.nationaltrust.org.uk/main/w-antony

Arbury Hall, Warwickshire CV10 7PT. Telephone: 02476 382804.
  Website: www.arburyestate.co.uk

Barwick Park, Yeovil, Somerset. Website: www.visitsouthsomerset.com
  (details of Follies Walk at Barwick)

Bicton, Exeter, Devon EX9 7BJ. Telephone: 01395 568465.
  Website: www.bictongardens.co.uk

Blenheim Palace, Woodstock, Oxfordshire OX20 1PP.
  Telephone: 01993 810530. Website: www.blenheimpalace.com

Boconnoc, Lostwithiel, Cornwall PL22 0RG. Telephone: 01208 872507.
  Website: www.boconnoc.com

Bramham Park, Wetherby, West Yorkshire LS23 6ND.
  Telephone: 01937 846000. Website: www.bramhampark.co.uk

Castle Ashby, Northampton NN7 1LQ. Telephone: 01604 695200.
  Website: www.castleashbygardens.co.uk

Castle Hill, South Molton, Devon EX32 0RH. Telephone: 01598 760336
  ext 1. Website: www.castlehilldevon.co.uk

Castle Howard, York YO60 7DA. Telephone: 01653 648333.
  Website: www.castlehoward.co.uk

Chatsworth House, Bakewell, Derbyshire DE45 1PP.
  Telephone: 01246 565300.
  Website: www.chatsworth.org

Chiswick House, Chiswick W4 2RP. Telephone: 020 8995 0508.
  Website: www.chgt.org.uk

Cirencester Park, Gloucestershire GL7 2BU. Telephone: 01285 653135.
Website: www.cirencesterpark.co.uk

Compton Verney, Warwickshire CV35 9HZ. Telephone: 01926 64500.
Website: www.comptonverney.org.uk

Croome Court, Worcestershire WR8 9JS. Telephone 01905 371006.
Website: www.nationaltrust.org.uk/croome

Endsleigh, Tavistock, Devon PL19 0PQ. Telephone: 01822 870000.
Website: www.hotelendsleigh.com

Farnborough Hall, Banbury OX17 1DU. Telephone: 01295 690002.
Website: www.nationaltrust.org.uk/main/w-farnboroughhall

Gibside, Gateshead, NE16 6BG. Telephone: 01207 541820.
Website: www.nationaltrust.org.uk/gibside

Greenway, Brixham, Devon TQ5 0ES. Telephone: 01803 842382.
Website: www.nationaltrust.org.uk/greenway

Hackfall, North Yorkshire HG4 3DE. Website: www.hackfall.org.uk

Hagley Hall, West Midlands DY9 9LG. Telephone: 01562 882408.
Website: www.hagleyhall.com

Hawkstone Park, Shrewsbury, Shropshire SY4 5UY.
Telephone: 01948 841700. Website: www.principal-
hayley.com/venues—hotels/hawkstone-park.aspx

Hestercombe, Taunton, Somerset TA2 8LG. Telephone: 01823 413923.
Website: hestercombe.com

Kedleston Hall, Derbyshire DE22 5JH. Telephone: 01332 842191.
Website: www.nationaltrust.org.uk/kedleston-hall

Mount Edgcumbe, Torpoint, Cornwall PL10 1HZ.
Telephone: 01752 822236. Website: www.mountedgcumbe.gov.uk

Painshill, Cobham, Surrey KT11 1JE. Telephone: 01932 584286.
Website: www.painshill.co.uk

Painswick Rococo Garden, Gloucestershire GL6 6TH.
Telephone: 01452 813204. Website: www.rococogarden.co.uk

Pentillie Castle, St Mellion, Saltash, Cornwall PL12 6QD.
Telephone: 01579 350044. Website: www.pentillie.co.uk

Port Eliot, St Germans, Saltash, Cornwall PL12 5ND.
Telephone: 01503 230211. Website: www.porteliot.co.uk

Prideaux Place, Padstow, Cornwall PL28 8RP. Telephone: 01841 532411.
Website: www.prideauxplace.co.uk

Prior Park, Bath BA2 5AH. Telephone: 01225 833422.
Website: www.nationaltrust.org.uk/priorpark

Rousham, Oxfordshire OX25 4QU. Telephone: 01689 347665.
Website: www.rousham.org

Royal Botanic Gardens, Kew, Richmond, Surrey TW9 3AB.
Telephone: 020 8332 5655. Website: www.kew.org

Saltram, Plympton, Plymouth, PL7 1UH. Telephone: 01752 333503.
Website: www.nationaltrust.org.uk/saltram

Shugborough, Milford, Staffordshire ST17 0XB. Telephone: 0845 459 8900/
01889 881388. Website: www.shugborough.org.uk

Stourhead, near Mere, Somerset BA12 6QD. Telephone: 01747 841152.
Website: www.nationaltrust.org.uk/stourhead

Stowe, Buckingham MK18 5EQ. Telephone: 01280 822850.
Website: www.nationaltrust.org.uk/stowe

Studley Royal, Fountains, Ripon, North Yorkshire HG4 3DY. Telephone:
01765 608888. Website: www.nationaltrust.org.uk/fountains-abbey

Wentworth Castle, Stainborough, Barnsley, South Yorkshire S75 3ET.
Telephone: 01226 776040. Website: www.wentworthcastle.org

Wentworth Woodhouse, South Yorkshire.
Website: www.wentworthvillage.net/monuments

West Wycombe Park, Buckinghamshire HP14 3AJ. Telephone: 01494
755571. Website: www.nationaltrust.org.uk/west-wycombe-park

Wimpole Hall, Royston, Cambridgeshire SG8 0BW. Telephone: 01223
206000. Website: www.nationaltrust.org.uk/wimpole

Woburn Abbey, Woburn Park, Bedfordshire MK17 9WA.
Telephone: 01525 290333. Website: www.woburn.co.uk

Wrest Park, Silsoe, Bedfordshire MK45 4HR. Telephone: 01525 860152.
Website: www.english-heritage.org.uk/daysout/properties/wrest-
park

WALES

Clytha Castle, near Abergavenny, Monmouthshire.
Telephone: 01628 825920. Website:
www.landmarktrust.org.uk/BuildingDetails/Overview/162/Clytha_
Castle (occasional open days)

Gnoll Country Park, Neath SA11 3BS. Telephone: 01639 635808.
Website: www.npt.gov.uk/gnollcountrypark

Hafod, Ceredigion, Wales. Telephone: 01974 282540.
Website:www.forestry.gov.uk/website/recreation.nsf/LUWebDocsBy
Key/WalesCeredigionNoForestHafod

Plas Newydd, Llangollen. Telephone: 01978 861314.
Website: www.llangollen.com/plas.html

The Kymin, Monmouth NP25 3SF. Telephone: 01600 719241.
Website: www.nationaltrust.org.uk/kymin

SCOTLAND

Blair Castle, Pitlochry, Perthshire PH18 5TL. Telephone: 01796 481207.
Website: www.blair-castle.co.uk

Chatelherault and Strathclyde Country Parks, Hamilton, Lanarkshire (the
    former High and Low Parks associated with Hamilton Palace).
    Website: www.visitlanarkshire.com
Culzean Castle, Maybole, Ayrshire & Arran KA19 8LE.
    Telephone: 0844 4932150.
    Website: www.nts.org.uk/property/culzean-castle-country-park
Dunmore Park ('The Pineapple'), Stirlingshire. (www.landmarktrust.org.uk)
Ossian's Cave and Hall at The Hermitage, Near Dunkeld, Perthshire PH8
    0HX. Telephone: 0844 4932192.
    Website: www.nts.org.uk/property/Hermitage
Penicuik House, near Edinburgh EH26 9LA. Telephone: 01383 872722.
    Website: www.penicuikhouse.co.uk

# GLOSSARY

This short glossary explains technical terms commonly used in the book;
additional terms will be found in M. Symes, *A Glossary of Garden History* (Shire,
2006) or *Pevsner's Architectural Glossary* (2010).

**Ashlar**
    Dressed stone worked to even faces and square edges used for the
    'polite' face of a building.
**Classical style**
    Architectural style derived from antique Greece and Rome, developed
    from the sixteenth century into styles such as Palladian and Baroque.
**Column**
    A tall pillar with an ornamental top or capital, common in Classical
    temples and porticoes; if free-standing often surmounted by a
    sculpture, at a distance from the house.
***Cottage ornée*** (French = ornamented cottage)
    A rustic building of picturesque design, popular in the late eighteenth
    and early nineteenth centuries.
**Eyecatcher**
    A feature placed to be seen from within or beyond the garden and park,
    often on an eminence and remote from the house.
***Ferme ornée*** (French = ornamented farm)
    Farmland surrounded by ornamental walks, enjoyed as part of the scenery.
**Gothick style**
    An architectural style based on medieval Gothic, with defining pointed
    arches, popular in Europe in the eighteenth century. It was lighter and
    more elegant and whimsical in its lines and decoration.

### Ha-ha

A sunken ditch between garden and park, invisible from the inner, garden side, to allow uninterrupted views of the park beyond, without allowing livestock into the garden. The inner face was revetted with a wall.

### Landscape garden

A garden on a large scale, naturalistic in appearance and disguising any regularity of design.

### Outlier

A feature in a remote part of the park or wider estate. A destination in a park circuit or an eyecatcher or both.

### Picturesque

Style of architecture and landscaping popular in the late eighteenth and early nineteenth century using irregular forms and textures and asymmetrical layouts forming attractive views.

### Pleasure ground

An informal area with lawns, ornamental plantings and architecture intended for walks, contrasting with the less intensively cultivated park enjoyed from horseback or horse-drawn transport and the more intensively cultivated flower and kitchen gardens.

Diagram of the
Parts of a Roman
Temple and
Columns

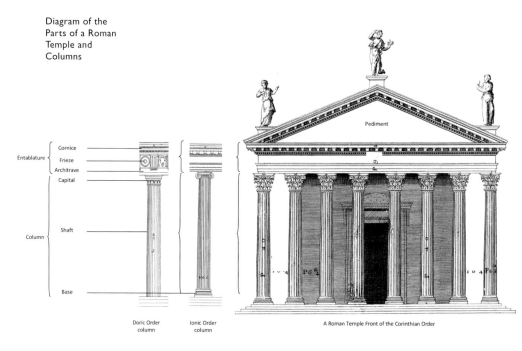

Entablature { Cornice
Frieze
Architrave

Capital

Column { Shaft

Base

Doric Order
column

Ionic Order
column

Pediment

A Roman Temple Front of the Corinthian Order

# INDEX